A **CAMPUSamerica** BOOK

GOD ON CAMPUS SACRED CAUSES & GLOBAL EFFECTS

TRENT SHEPPARD
Afterword by PETE GREIG

IVP Books

An imprint of InterVarsity Press
Downers Grove, Illinois

InterVarsity Press
P.O. Box 1400, Downers Grove, IL 60515-1426
World Wide Web: www.ivpress.com
E-mail: email@ivpress.com

InterVarsity Press® is the book-publishing division of InterVarsity Christian Fellowship/ USA®, a student movement active on campus at hundreds of universities, colleges and schools of nursing in the United States of America, and a member movement of the International Fellowship of Evangelical Students. For information about local and regional activities, write Public Relations Dept., InterVarsity Christian Fellowship/USA, 6400 Schroeder Rd., P.O. Box 7895, Madison, WI 53707-7895, or visit the IVCF website at <www.intervarsity.org>.

All Scripture quotations, unless otherwise indicated, are taken from the Holy Bible, New Living Translation, *copyright ©1996. Used by permission of Tyndale House Publishers, Inc., Wheaton, Illinois 60189. All rights reserved.*

Design: Cindy Kiple
Images: iStockphoto

ISBN 978-0-8308-3631-4

Printed in the United States of America ∞

InterVarsity Press is committed to protecting the environment and to the responsible use of natural resources. As a member of Green Press Initiative we use recycled paper whenever possible. To learn more about the Green Press Initiative, visit <www.greenpressinitiative.org>.

Library of Congress Cataloging-in-Publication Data

Sheppard, Trent, 1975-
  God on campus: sacred causes and global effects / Trent Sheppard.
      p. cm.
  Includes bibliographical references.
  ISBN 978-0-8308-3631-4 (pbk.: alk. paper)
  1. College students—Religious life. 2. Universities and
colleges—Religion. 3. Prayer—Christianity. I. Title.
BV4531.3.S545 2009
248.8'34—dc22

                                                                    2009032080

P	18	17	16	15	14	13	12	11	10	9	8	7	6	5	4	3	2	1
Y	23	22	21	20	19	18	17	16	15	14	13	12	11	10	09			

For Bronwyn,

my epiphany of prayer and the poor.

And for my parents,

Glenn and Jackie Sheppard,

who taught me how to pray

and gave me a love for history.

CONTENTS

PART THREE: *LIVING FAITH*

INTRODUCTION

*Who, then, can help the religious soul in the great universities,
the soul that craves the freedom of full being?*

—CHARLES MALIK

Maybe, like me, you've heard stories about a time when the soul of
our great universities intentionally engaged with God. When Harvard
was considered a holy place and Princeton trained prophets. When
students and professors could not help but pray because there were
certain questions that could only be answered by an intellect greater
than our own. When honest faith was viewed not as a religious crutch
but as a rational response to an unimaginably complex and purposeful cosmos.

The stunning achievements of the modern world, however, challenged that view. "I put up my thumb and shut one eye," remarked
Neil Armstrong when he walked on the moon, "and my thumb blotted
out the planet Earth." Perspective is a powerful thing, particularly
when you're standing on the moon. Surely it is what Armstrong said
next, though, that more precisely puts the human view, regardless of
where we're standing, in proper perspective. "I didn't feel like a gi-
ant," he confessed, "I felt very, very small."

Human achievements take on different meaning when viewed
through the vast lens of an ever-unfurling universe. Humility, in fact,
almost comes naturally when we are awestruck. In those rare and
sometimes frightening moments of astonishment—when an astro-

naut helps us see the cosmos a bit more clearly or a raging hurricane unmercifully batters the concrete levees of a city until they snap like crayons in the hands of an angry child—we turn again to God and remember how very small humans really are. Prayer, then, is finally nothing more than the honest confession of a humble person.

Campus America—which is an abbreviated way of saying: *every college and university campus in the United States*—is at a moment of profound potential. Why? Because people are praying. People are engaging with God again. The soul of our "great universities" is beginning to stir. Students and professors, young and old, the powerful and the poor: each in their own way are seeking for something more solid than the shaky commitment of the stock market, something more lasting than the wonderful but fragile ideals of democracy, something immeasurably more sacred than a "Christian" nation.

The United States is waking up from the American Dream to a world of debt, and there is a renewed national desire to redefine what we mean when we refer to ourselves as a "great nation." It is not that America is done dreaming but that the students of the United States—and so many young people from other nations who come here to study—are yearning for something much bigger than the American Dream. And that is probably why some friends and I started to have some dreams of our own.

CONSIDERING THE ACCENT OF GOD

All [people] dream: but not equally. Those who dream by night in the dusty recesses of their minds wake in the day to find that it was vanity: but the dreamers of the day are dangerous [people], for they may act their dream with open eyes, to make it possible.

—T. E. LAWRENCE, *SEVEN PILLARS OF WISDOM*

"Campus America," said the voice, jolting my English friend Pete

Greig awake, "Call Campus America to pray!" It was January 23, 2005. Although Pete could not tell if the voice was inner or audible, either way it had awakened him from a deep sleep and shot a surge of adrenaline through his entire body. Unable to shake the feeling that God was speaking to him, he quietly climbed out of bed—careful not to disturb Dave, who was sound asleep on the other side of the hotel room—and made his way downstairs to the lobby. Blurry-eyed and buzzing with an awareness of God, Pete rubbed the sleep out of his eyes, asked for a pen from the hotel desk attendant and started to record in his journal what was happening.

It was as if God had a dream for the students of the United States. A dream that would only be realized in and through prayer. A dream that had awakened this Englishman in California from the dead of sleep.

Call Campus America to pray.

Now it must be understood that prayer was not really a new thing for Pete. In early autumn 1999, he and some friends in England experimented with the idea of trying to pray nonstop for a month. They did it by praying in shifts—in between working and studying, sleeping and eating—all of them taking turns in a homemade prayer room at their church in Chichester, England. Pete recounts what happened in that first prayer room in *Red Moon Rising*, a book which tracks the 24-7 Prayer movement from its unassuming beginnings in the south of England to a global community of mission and justice that is still praying continuously to this day.

Call Campus America to pray.

On that early winter morning in a hotel lobby in California, Pete became keenly aware that God was planning something significant for young people studying in the United States. He knew this represented something broader than the emerging 24-7 Prayer network of which he was a part. And he also knew that prayer was not the end goal; rather, it was just the beginning. Uttering a simple prayer and closing his journal, Pete went to tell his friend Dave about what he had just experienced.

Now, if you are anything like me, you can't help but wonder what sort of accent God would have used to awaken this Englishman. Surely it must have been British, right? Because that is the primary culture through which Pete learned the English language and obviously the most natural way an Englishman would hear from God. Thus if God spoke those same words to someone from Egypt, surely the words would be in Arabic, right? To someone from China, Mandarin or Cantonese, right? To someone from Fiji, Fijian, right?

When considering the accent of God, we must remember that the Being who created the cosmos and everything in it is not bound by culture or language or accent. In the letter to the Galatians, the apostle Paul said it like this: "There is no longer Jew or Gentile. . . . For you are all one in Christ Jesus" (Galatians 3:28). Perhaps an Englishman heard "Call Campus America to pray" because God wants to assure us that what is coming to U.S. campuses is not limited to the United States. God's dream is much bigger than the American Dream.

REGARDING LETHARGIC FOOTBALL AND RAISING THE DEAD

We had better . . . take seriously the witness of the entire
early church, that Jesus of Nazareth was raised . . . to a
new sort of life, . . . and that his followers in being the
witnesses to these things were . . . commissioned to take
the news of his victory to the ends of the earth.

N. T. WRIGHT, *THE CHALLENGE OF JESUS*

When Pete returned to his hotel room that morning, he discovered Dave was still asleep and decided to take a quick shower before waking him. While in the shower, Pete again had the distinct sense God was communicating with him. There was no ray of light, descending angels, an unusually deep voice or anything of that sort at all. Rather, Pete simply had a calm but very acute awareness that Dave had just awakened from a significant dream of his own. By the time Pete stepped out of the bathroom, Dave was sitting upright in his bed and journaling furiously. Similar to Pete's experience from a few hours earlier, Dave had been awakened by what seemed to be God communicating with him as well.

It's time to call the dead to get into the game.

As if the mystifying words were planted into the fertile landscape of his mind from the first moment he opened his eyes that morning, Dave could not shake the sense God was with him in the hotel room. Furthermore, he was convinced the words *It's time to call the dead to get into the game* had something to do with American campuses. (At that point, mind you, Dave had no idea what Pete had experienced.) Like a scene from a film recently rewound and now ready to roll again, the dream Dave had just awakened from started to replay in his mind.

He could see himself walking out of the sanctuary of a church building and getting ready to watch a college football game that was about to begin. Strangely enough, the entire football team was waiting in the church lobby. Dave spotted an old friend—dressed in full gear for the game, with all the pads and right equipment—but completely unprepared to play. He had a vacant look in his eyes and appeared lethargic, as if he were dead even though he seemed alive. What was especially significant to Dave, though, is that the old friend he saw, a young man he knew from high school, had actually died during their senior year.

It's time to call the dead to get into the game.

As Pete and Dave discussed their unusual morning, comparing their journal entries and praying together, they both became increasingly convinced that God was indeed planning something unique for Campus America. Whatever it was (and that precise point was not yet entirely clear), prayer was the way to prepare for it. And some sort of resurrection—a stunning biblical theme that stretches from Ezekiel's army of dry bones to the bodily resurrection of Jesus himself—was part of the unfolding plan.

N. T. Wright, Anglican bishop and New Testament historian, has

written about the earliest followers of Jesus' understanding of resurrection and how central it was to their faith. "They believed," explains
Wright in *Surprised by Hope*, "that God was going to do for the whole
cosmos what he had done for Jesus at Easter." This early Christian conviction is clearly echoed in Paul's letter to the Romans: "With eager
hope, the creation looks forward to the day when it will join God's children in glorious freedom from death and decay" (Romans 8:20-21).

What that means is this:

- **Following Jesus is much more than a religious conversion.**

- **Following Jesus is about *new creation*.**

- **God not only intends to save our souls.**

- **God intends to *remake our humanity*.**

Sin corrupted our original design as the image-bearers of God and
distorted our primary calling as the caretakers of the cosmos. This is
why there is suffering in the world. Humans have endured profound
pain because of sin—for whenever there is a lack of love, there is suffering too—and our planet has been abused terribly as a result. Jesus
came to deal with the deadly corruption of sin by dying the death our
unloving choices lead to and then rising again to incorruptible life.
The good news is that God has welcomed us to join the resurrected
Jesus in this new way of being human. It is time, indeed, to call the
dead to get into the game.

A TALKING HORSE AND A STUDENT STAMPEDE

*Then instantly the pale brightness of the mist and the
fiery brightness of the Lion rolled themselves together
into a swirling glory and gathered themselves up and
disappeared.*

—C. S. LEWIS, *THE HORSE AND HIS BOY*

It was a few days later when Pete called me in England to recount
what had happened to him and Dave in California. Although I am an

American by birth, I had been living in the United Kingdom for seven years at that point, helping to lead a small community of college-age young people called The Factory, part of Youth With A Mission. As my friend Pete told me about his unusual encounter with God and what it might mean for the campuses of America, tears started to collect in the corner of my eyes, and before long were making a wet path down my face. Pete stopped talking when he realized I was weeping.

There are some things so deep inside us that it is difficult to find words for them:

- **The wonder of a baby being born to parents who have lost a child.**
- **The frustration of being misunderstood by someone you respect.**
- **The grief of a dear friend dying.**
- **The mystery of falling in love.**

The calling of God can be like that.

Pete's story had not evoked such raw emotion in me. It was what Pete did not know about my story: the long journey I had been on as it related to campuses and calling, broken prayers of surrender and the disillusioned hope of a student movement. For years, it seemed, I had been trying the best I knew how to make something happen, but it never worked out the way I wanted. Somewhere along the way, in that lonely and important place between believing in the unseen and learning to be honest about the unknown, my wearied dreams of a student awakening had started to die. So when Pete told me his story, it touched the raw nerve of my own story. That is why I cried.

Reflecting on the conversation with Pete sometime later and thinking about my journey as it related to campuses and the question of calling, I told my fiancée, Bronwyn, that I felt a little like Jacob after he wrestled with the angel. I was limping from the fight, but closer to God because of it. Even though Bronwyn and I did not yet know what our new lives together would hold, we were certain we wanted God to guide our steps wherever they led. And that is why one night on the phone, having talked with Bronwyn again about my strange and teary conversation with Pete, she prayed this simple prayer for me: "Lord, please speak to Trent in his dreams tonight. Amen."

Now it is important to understand that I do not have a background in any sort of "spiritual" dreaming. Although I was deeply moved by Pete's experience and Dave's dream in California, my subconscious musings at night usually have no point at all (although they do at times involve me jumping unusually high). So when Bronwyn asked God to give me a dream, I seriously did not expect it to happen, and I certainly did not have faith that it would. To be honest, all I did was close my eyes and go to sleep.

When I opened my eyes, however, I was standing in an open field and there was an unmistakable rumbling rising from the ground. The earth itself was trembling, as was I, because I was afraid. I was fearful of where that pounding sound was coming from and frightfully aware I was about to discover its planet-shaking source. Listening more carefully, I realized the wild sound was gathering momentum and, in fact, coming closer. The dirt beneath me began to dance with a frenzied fury.

Gazing across the open field, I was confronted by the cause of the untamed and thunderous sound as a wild stampede of animals rushed into my view. There were so many of them, and the mythical beasts were of such marvelous variety, that the uncontrollable fear I had once felt was soon replaced by sheer wonder. Like a scene from J. R. R. Tolkien's *Lord of the Rings* or a glimpse into C. S. Lewis's Chronicles of Narnia, the animals were supernatural in appearance: lions that talked, horses more powerful than any I had ever seen, noble buffaloes that roared.

I was completely captivated by what I was witnessing and so stunned by how close the animals were that I dared not move. It was then that one of them, a wild and courageous horse with two majestic horns, saw me and charged. In my dream I immediately knew three things about this raging mare: she was a university student, she was disillusioned by religion, and she was very angry. (I cannot explain why I knew these particular things about the horse, nor can I explain why I also innately knew the enraged mare would understand me if I talked with her. In the dream, I just knew.)

"Please," I cried out, "let me explain!" While I ran for shelter, the horse continued to charge relentlessly. I frantically tried to explain that I too had been burned by religion and disillusioned by empty spirituality. Nearing the tree, the mare finally seemed to understand what I was so desperate to explain and rather than trampling me, she knelt down on the ground beside me. By this point the horse was so wearied with running that it was hard for her to stand. As the wild stampede of animals continued to pound their way through the open field, I looked into the mare's eyes and asked her name.

I am Storm Gathering.

Opening my eyes to the light of morning, the open field and fearless horse were nowhere to be found. I slipped out of bed, with the student stampede still thundering through my mind, got down on my knees and asked God what the dream meant. It was simple. A student movement was indeed coming to the campuses of America. And a large part of that movement would be made up of young people who were disillusioned by certain elements of their religious backgrounds and desperately searching for a faith that was wildly courageous, intellectually honest, socially engaged and genuinely free.

I am Storm Gathering.

This raging mare, with her two majestic horns, represented a dynamic and engaging faith that bridged the modern divide that so often separates the sacred and the secular. To her, life was not about one or the other—the physical or the spiritual—it was about both. Storm Gathering was committed to prayer *and* the poor, intimacy with God *and* advocacy for the outcast, freedom from her own sins *and* freedom for the world's slaves. Her unfettered faith was attempting to reclaim the ancient words of the prophet Isaiah, that earthy description of true holiness by which Jesus defined his ministry:

> The Spirit of the Lord is upon me,
> for he has anointed me
> to bring Good News to the poor.

He has sent me to proclaim that captives will be released,
that the blind will see,
that the oppressed will be set free,
    and that the time of the Lord's favor has come. (Luke 4:18-19;
see Isaiah 61:1-2)

The movement of prayer currently building across the campuses of America must be worked out in practical faith—a faith that makes sense to students and professors, parents and teachers, plumbers and scientists, architects and flight attendants—or else the movement will die as quickly as it comes. "So here's what I want you to do," Paul says in Romans, "God helping you: Take your everyday, ordinary life—your sleeping, eating, going-to-work, and walking-around life—and place it before God as an offering" (Romans 12:1 *The Message*). The goal is not for us to abandon our studies in economics or education, for example, and become preachers instead. The goal is to live like Jesus in the very soul of society.

History alone will judge the faithfulness of our response to this calling. We will not be judged by how many people we pack into our prayer rooms or by how many converts we can record. Rather, history will judge our generation by whether or not the fruit we produce is the sort that lasts. Some dreams, like trees, are destined to die simply because they do not have roots deep enough to live. Other dreams, like Dr. Martin Luther King's, may take a long time to grow into fullness, but their lasting effect is historic.

That is the sort of dreaming required for our day. Generous dreams that freely merge the great divide between the powerful and the poor. Broken dreams that understand what it practically means to sacrificially give our lives away in the service of others. Holy dreams that are not bound by sacred rooms or limited to mystical experiences (or even to talking horses, for that matter), but the sort of dreams that are set free to reimagine what a redeemed humanity might truly be in everyday, extraordinary life. That is what this book is about. And that is how simple prayers and sacred dreams, daring plans and practical faith help to shape the outworking of history.

THE NARRATIVE OF HISTORY AND THE PART WE MUST PLAY

Truth is not abstract ideas or mystical experiences, but a story of what God has done.

—LESSLIE NEWBIGIN

Thomas Cahill, in his insightful book *The Gifts of the Jews*, explains that the ancient Hebrews understood time as an unfolding story of destiny, rather than as a never-ending circle of fate. Unlike most other religions and philosophies of a similar era, which viewed time as a recurring cycle predetermined by the gods, the Hebrews believed that history was a living narrative that was dynamically moving toward a grand and glorious conclusion. "This great, overwhelming movement, exemplified in the [early biblical] stories," Cahill explains, "makes history real to the human consciousness for the first time—with the future really dependant on what I do in the present."

The stories and teachings of the Hebrew Bible were more than religious documents to the ancient Jews. Rather, the Bible was sacred history they had participated in with God. Because of their narrative understanding of time, the Bible was the book that invited them to real and responsible engagement with the needs of their community and the challenges of their world. To read the Bible in the way it was originally intended, therefore, and to faithfully respond to what it teaches us today, we must learn how to approach life as holy history that is still in the making. Now that certainly does not mean we will be adding new books to the Bible, but it does mean that we do have an important part to play in determining where history is heading now.

The remarkable story of college and university students in the United States is an enduring history of faith and education, holy rebellion and student prayer that extends even further back than the nation's founding. We must remember that Harvard was established in 1636, a full 140 years before America's Declaration of Independence was signed by the founding fathers in 1776. This means that *the stu-*

dents of the United States have as much responsibility as the government of the United States in determining the direction of the nation.

You may feel young, Campus America, *but you have been here a very long time.*

This is a book to help you remember your roots, to remind you of the sacred stories and global effects that have been part of the history of campuses in America from the very beginning. This is a book that tells the stories of ordinary people like you and me—bold and timid, brilliant and insecure, disillusioned and dangerous, ambitious and naive, holy and fallen, fearless and afraid—people who prayed, people who conspired together with their friends in faith and action, people who believed their lives could actually help shape the unfolding narrative of history.

This is your story.
This is your history.
And you do have a part to play.

Part One

CAMPUS FOUNDATIONS

What else can save us but your hand

remaking what you have made?

—SAINT AUGUSTINE

1

Massachusetts Bay Colony, 1654. *Nights in New England can be unmercifully cold, particularly in that unpredictable period between late autumn and early winter when overly eager clouds have already carpeted the earth with snow.*

The forty-four-year-old professor, who looked much older than he actually was, rubbed his hands together to keep them warm, while he stared at the dimming embers in his fireplace and wondered what the court would decide. Henry Dunster, Harvard's first president, had been charged with heresy.

Because of the seriousness of his crime and the unyielding rule of the court, there was no longer any question whether Dunster would continue overseeing the young college. The critical question that plagued his mind at present was whether or not the authorities would allow him and his family to stay in their home throughout the upcoming winter. For even though Dunster had constructed the house at his own expense, the residence was on college property.

Turning over a charred log in the fireplace, Dunster again glanced at the letter of appeal he had written earlier that evening. There, on a rough wooden table built by his own hands, rested the plain parchment on which he had outlined for the Massachusetts General Court multiple reasons why his young and vulnerable family needed a few months reprieve before they were forced to move. Dunster's wife and youngest child were ill, clearly not healthy enough to endure a search for new lodging at this brutal time of year.

Watching the fire fade from crimson red to chalky ash, and fretting over the fearful implications for his family resulting from his banishment, the disgraced president reflected on his fourteen years of service at Harvard. Dunster's memories were many that cold November night, but foremost in his mind were two particular recollections, one of a sacred commencement service and the other of a holy rebellion.

It was September 23, 1642, Harvard's first graduation day. Unlike Dunster's own commencement service at Cambridge University in England, the nine young men before him now were standing instead of kneeling. President Dunster and the college overseers had decided that God alone was worthy of the bended knee and thus these Harvard men of the New World would receive their Book of Arts standing tall.

The president looked each candidate in the eye before addressing the congregation, a crowd primarily composed of the educated men of the colony, in Latin:

> *Honorandi veri, vosque Reverendi Presbyteri, praesento vobis hosce Juvenes, quos scio tam Doctrina quam moribus idoneos esse as primum in Artibus gradum suscipiendum, pro more Academiarum in Anglia.*

> *Honorable Gentlemen and Reverend Ministers I present to you these youths, whom I know to be sufficient in knowledge as in manners to be raised to the First Degree in Arts, according to the customs of the Universities in England.*

Most of the proceedings that day were conducted in Latin, with the occasional presentation in Greek or Hebrew as well, as was fitting for scholars. In fact, even the extemporaneous and long-winded opening prayer of Reverend Thomas Shepard was delivered in Latin, in which the minister especially gave thanks for the "godly learning" of the first graduating class of "this School of the Prophets."

President Dunster had plenty of reasons to be proud of his Harvard men on that autumn commencement day, for these graduates represented a new era of faith and learning for the Massachusetts Bay Colony, and indeed, for the New World as a whole. Calling each of the candidates by name, the president charged the nine young "prophets" with their sacred responsibility:

> *Tibique trado hunc librum una cum potestate publice praelegendi, in aliqua Artium quam profiteris, quotiescunque ad hoc munus evocatus fueris.*

> *I hand thee this book, together with the power to lecture pub-*

licly in any one of the arts which thou hast studied, whensoever thou shalt have been called to that office.

Dunster entrusted the scholars with the "power to lecture publicly" because their education was meant to benefit the community as a whole. Their acquired skills and classical learning were not simply for personal gain, but for civic service as ministers and professional leaders of society. The president wanted these honored graduates to understand they now had a holy obligation, before God, to seek and always teach veritas—the Latin word for "truth"—regardless of what consequences may come.

President Dunster and the college overseers knew it was an important moment for the young colony and a vital step forward in the Puritan dream of pioneering a New World. Harvard's first commencement service continued throughout the remainder of the day and was completed with a hearty New England meal served on wooden trenchers and washed down with malty college beer.

More than a decade later, having led Harvard through an extraordinary stretch of early development that meant graduates of this colonial wilderness college were considered equal in academic merit to scholars from the great universities of Oxford and Cambridge, Henry Dunster experienced a crisis of faith. His dilemma had to do with the question of infant baptism, a vitally important affair in Puritan New England.

According to official church doctrine and the civil law of Massachusetts, parents were required to have their children baptized shortly after they were born. A rebellious sect, however, had begun teaching that baptism was only for believers who had chosen the sacrament for themselves, not for newborn babes. These "baptist heretics" ignited a blaze of controversy in New England with their nonconformist ideas, and the Puritan authorities had accordingly banished them from Massachusetts in an attempt to calm the social unrest.

What specifically drew Dunster into this dangerous debate was a court case against three dissenting ministers, who even though they had been exiled to Rhode Island, made their way back to Massachusetts to visit a fellow believer and to baptize several new converts.

Upon being caught by the local authority, the three men were publicly tried for their crime.

The charge against them, as articulated by Reverend John Cotton, a respected Boston minister who advised the General Court, was particularly serious because "denying infant baptism would overthrow all." The church was the essential stabilizing force in Puritan society and to openly challenge its authority, especially about an issue so vital to the spiritual life of families in the community, explained Reverend Cotton, made these men guilty of a "capital offence" as "soul murderers."

The governor, Mr. John Endecott, told the dissenting Baptists "you deserve to die," but he passed a sentence against them of heavy fines or "to be well whipped" instead. Two of the accused men, Dr. Clarke and Mr. Crandall, had their fines paid through the generosity of friends. The third defendant, a man named Obadiah Holmes, refused to pay his fine, however, and was brutally beaten at the public whipping post instead.

Administered with a tri-band leather whip, the thirty stripes received across the bare back of Obadiah Holmes were only ten lashes shy of a death sentence. Even though his wounds were so severe he was forced to rest on his elbows and knees for weeks thereafter because he could not "suffer any part of his body to touch the bed whereon he lay," he told the magistrates after his whipping, "You have struck me as with roses."

For President Dunster, the harsh fines and bloody beating of the Rhode Island Baptists precipitated a soul-searching quest for veritas as it related to the issue of infant baptism. Was dissenting against this doctrine deserving of so serious a punishment? And, for that matter, was the Bible altogether clear about this doctrine anyway?

The president of Harvard, heedless of the social and religious implications it might mean, began a thorough examination of Scripture and of various theological writings about baptism to discover the truth. If he had charged his young scholars to seek and teach veritas, Dunster reasoned with God in prayer, how could he do any less?

After much study and prayerful thought, the president could find no biblical warrant for the civil law that insisted on infant baptism. His crisis of faith came about because he was committed to public truth. Henry Dunster's conscience would simply not allow him to remain silent on an issue that had caused others to suffer.

In an act of holy rebellion that would dramatically alter his life and ultimately lead to his downfall as Harvard's president, Dunster began preaching from the pulpit against the civil necessity of infant baptism. When his fourth child was born in 1653, he refused to have the baby baptized on the grounds of conscience. A heated public debate, in which his friends and colleagues desperately sought to convince the president of his error, continued for some months before Henry Dunster was finally dismissed from his presidency and banished from the colony.

A cold draft, creeping through the side sealing of a window near the front door of the president's house, stirred Dunster from the intensity of his memories. The fire was almost out now and his heart was too tired to reflect any further on his fall. Glancing again at the letter of appeal on his table, the wearied president whispered a simple prayer for his family, especially asking God to grant compassion to the court.

Although his decision to challenge the church's doctrine was undoubtedly costly, Dunster had determined the choice was worth it nonetheless. For that was what his commitment to veritas required of him and that was why Harvard had been founded in the first place: "to advance Learning and perpetuate it to Posterity" so as not "to leave an illiterate Ministry to the Churches, when our present Ministers shall lie in the Dust."*

---

*This narrative of the history that led to President Dunster's dismissal in 1654 is a fictionalized version and was especially inspired by "The Harvard Heretic" in Diane Rapaport, *The Naked Quaker: True Crimes and Controversies from the Courts of Colonial New England*, and also by Jeremiah Chaplin, *Life of Henry Dunster*, and Samuel Morison, *The Founding of Harvard College*. The final quotation is from a 1643 document titled *New Englands First Fruits*, which contains the earliest account of Harvard College. Those same words are still engraved on a stone tablet outside the entrance of Harvard today.

HARVARD'S FIRST HERETIC

A HISTORY OF HOLY REBELLION

I am not the man you take me to be.

—HENRY DUNSTER

Harvard had a rough start. Not only did the college overseers dismiss the first president as a heretic but the earliest master of the college, a man named Nathaniel Eaton, was fired for beating his assistant with a walnut bat "big enough to have killed a horse." (At least that was how Reverend Thomas Shepard described the wooden cudgel in his deposition of the incident in 1638.) To be fair to Master Eaton, though, it was not simply his tendency toward flogging that led to his eventual firing, but also a series of grave accusations that his wife starved the students, skimped on their beer and occasionally slipped goat's dung into their pudding as well. (And you thought *your* college food was bad?)

The little details of history are important. They help us laugh at the quirkiness of our humanity and keep us mindful of the peculiar acts of madness that occasionally result in a moment of greatness: If Master Eaton had never been fired, then President Dunster may never have been hired and history might still be waiting for Harvard's first heretic. In a generation addicted to the immediacy of the Internet, however, the discipline of seeking ancient treasure between the crumbling covers of an old book sometimes seems boring. Unfortunately, history has a bad rap these days.

In the hidden details of time, though, the twisting and turning narrative of our collective human memory, we discover the remarkable (and often bizarre) similarities we share with those who have gone before us. For while much has changed since Harvard was founded in the seventeenth century, some things are undoubtedly still the same, like the burning urge to rebel against oppressive ideas that enslave people instead of setting them free. Indeed, that may be one of the most powerful lessons we can learn from history: *There are some things worth rebelling against.*

We are taught this simple and profound truth from the stories of people like Rosa Parks and Desmond Tutu, people who looked oppression in the eye and determined it was better to suffer in peaceful revolt than to stay silent in the face of evil. Keeping quiet, of course, is usually a much safer option (at least for a while, that is), but the God of the Bible does not necessarily call us to safety. On the contrary, the sovereign yet vulnerable God we see in Jesus—the God who was crucified—calls us to engage with injustice, even when it is costly.

It is challenging for our modern minds to understand why President Dunster's preaching against infant baptism caused such controversy in old New England. Dunster's actions were not only scandalous to those who heard about it but were actually dangerous for him and his family. It had barely been three years since Obadiah Holmes was publicly beaten for the same sort of dissent. To grasp the weighty significance of Henry Dunster's risky decision and to start wrestling with the issues worth rebelling against in our own time, we should begin our journey by having a look at the surprising history of holy rebellion out of which Harvard's first heretic emerged.*

---

*In case you were wondering, President Dunster and his family were given a few months reprieve after his 1654 letter of appeal to the court, granting them until March 1655 to vacate Harvard's property. After he left the college, Henry Dunster preached for a few years in the nearby Plymouth Colony and then died of natural causes in 1659. His body was brought back to the college and laid to rest in the Old Burying Ground in Harvard Square.

A PROFESSOR'S REVOLT

My conscience is captive to the word of God.

—MARTIN LUTHER*

Thinking deeply and acting accordingly is a dangerous thing to do. Just ask Martin Luther, the "solitary professor" who "faced, without flinching" the power structures of his time "in the name of the Word of God." When considering the Reformation, that history-splitting theological and social earthquake that cut across an empire and divided a continent, we must remember it was not a politician's speech that sparked the revolution but a professor's ninety-five theses.

Martin Luther (1483–1546) was a Catholic monk and professor of theology who lived in a critical phase of history. It was an era in which the controlling traits of medieval theology were beginning to be challenged by the expanding ideas of modern thought. Worldviews were shifting and people were starting to question the fundamental "facts" about God they had been taught. When Martin Luther nailed his ninety-five theses to the church door in Wittenberg in 1517, ideas that challenged the authority of the Holy Roman Empire and paved the way to a renewed engagement with the mind, this revolutionary professor was inviting people to a public debate about the Bible.

Now, before we explore the extraordinary effect of Luther's reform on the church and how it influenced certain thinkers at Cambridge in England (which in turn resulted in the founding of Harvard in New England), allow me first to offer an inadequate but genuine word of sorrow to my Jewish friends, and many others of various backgrounds, whose ancestors have suffered profoundly at the hands of Protestant Christians. Martin Luther wrote inexcusably hateful things about Jews, words that were used against the Jewish people as recently as

---

*Luther's complete quote at the Diet of Worms, where he was on trial for heresy in 1521: "Unless I am convinced by the testimony of the Scriptures or by clear reason . . . I am bound by the Scriptures I have quoted and my conscience is captive to the Word of God. I cannot and will not retract anything, since it is neither safe nor right to go against conscience. I cannot do otherwise; here I stand; may God help me."

the Nazi regime. What's more, Protestant believers have long been guilty of justifying violence in the name of God: a God, mind you, who looks very different than the One we see in Jesus. While we cannot change history, we must be honest about our past. Christianity has blood on its hands. And the only way we may be able to be reconciled with those we have wounded and find forgiveness for the unthinkable crimes we have committed—many of those crimes in the name of Jesus, God forgive us!—is to begin the humiliating journey of openness. Christians, more than most, are in dire need of the grace that comes though humility. In chapter three, we will look at this issue more deeply as it relates to the original sins of "Christian" America—broken treaties and the slave trade—but for now, we will return to Cambridge.

EMMANUEL COLLEGE AND THE ACORN OF CAMBRIDGE

They were determined to found a new Cambridge as well as a New England.

—SAMUEL MORISON

About fifty years after Professor Luther nailed his ninety-five ideas to the church door in Wittenberg, another professor, Thomas Cartwright, attempted to take Luther's Continental reform even further at Cambridge University. In 1570 Cartwright gave a controversial series of lectures that contrasted the leadership structure of the Church of England with the leadership model in the book of Acts. The essential point of Cartwright's teaching was to communicate that state government (i.e., Queen Elizabeth I and the Parliament of England) should not have authority over local church government (i.e., congregations should determine for themselves how they would be led).

The effect was extraordinary. Professor Cartwright was ultimately fired from the university, a warrant for his arrest was soon thereafter issued, and many Cambridge students opted against wearing the clerical academic robes that identified them with the Church of England. (Collegiate fashion, one should understand, was different in the 1500s than it is today.) Cartwright's teaching was part of an emerging church movement called Puritanism, basically a vocal and very strong-willed group of people in the Anglican Church who felt the English Reformation had not gone far enough in its purifying revolt against the Church of Rome. Because of the compelling lectures of Professor Cartwright and others like him, Cambridge quickly became one of the white-hot centers of Puritan reform in sixteenth-century England.

A few years after Professor Cartwright's dismissal, a college called Emmanuel was founded at Cambridge University. Because Emmanuel College was so deeply steeped in Puritanism from its very beginning, Queen Elizabeth remarked to its founder, Sir Walter Mildmay, "I hear that you have erected a Puritan foundation." To which Sir Walter evasively replied, "No, Madam, far be it from me to countenance any thing contrary to your established laws, but I have set an acorn, which, when it becomes an oak, God alone knows what will be the fruit thereof." And so the seed was planted (in the fertile roots of holy rebellion) for the eventual founding of Harvard, as the majority of the early Puritan scholars who settled New England were graduates of Emmanuel College, Cambridge University.

RETURNING TO OUR ROOTS

Truth is not only that which awaits discovery,
but also that which was once known and is now
threatened by forgetfulness.

—ROBERT FONG

Puritan pioneers of the Massachusetts General Court founded Harvard in 1636. The college was originally described as the "School of the Prophets" because, "according to a medieval tradition," explains Harvard historian Samuel Morison, "the prophet Samuel presided over the world's first university." The school received its proper name in 1638 when minister John Harvard left his entire library and a generous endowment of £779 to the young "wilderness college" upon his death.

In the College Laws of 1642, written under the able leadership of President Henry Dunster, the original purpose of Harvard is stated simply:

> Let every student be plainly instructed and earnestly pressed to consider well the main end of his life and studies is to know God and Jesus Christ which is eternal life, John 17:3, and therefore to lay Christ in the bottom, as the only foundation of all sound knowledge and learning. And seeing the Lord giveth wisdom, let everyone seriously set himself by prayer, in secret, to seek it of Him.

Imagine that—God and Harvard in some sort of sacred pact from the very beginning: a holy conspiracy of education and conviction woven into the earliest foundations of America's original college.

Obviously much has changed since Harvard was founded, and change is certainly not a negative thing. During Harvard's early era, Latin was the only language allowed on campus unless there was a specific presentation assigned in English. The library then largely comprised 320 donated volumes, whereas Harvard's library today has more than sixteen million books. The original endowment from the General Court was £400 in 1636, which combined with John Harvard's £779 in 1638, made for a sizable amount of cash in the seventeenth century. Harvard's endowment in 2008, in comparison, was $36.9 billion. Clearly, change can be a really good thing.

With the remarkable reputation and intellectual influence Harvard has gained in the last 370 years, however, also comes profound responsibility and tremendous temptation. President Dunster foresaw this dilemma when he warned his students, "Take heed . . . lest desiring to be as gods, we become as devils." The power of knowledge, as the opening chapters of Genesis so poetically remind us, can be used for good and evil.

When writing of Harvard and the campuses of America *returning to their roots*, please do not misunderstand me. The point is not that there would be some sort of Puritan uprising to take Harvard back. (Surely the image of a posse of militant seventeenth-century ministers, dressed in black-and-white camouflage, with the Bible in one hand and an antique musket in the other, stealthily scaling the ivy towers of our campuses is more frightening than it is inspiring.) Rather, the point is that students and professors, engaged parents and concerned presidents would begin creating some sacred space on campus to engage with God again.

In the words of the late Jaroslav Pelikan, Sterling Professor of History at Yale, "Knowledge and virtue are not identical, and the expulsion of ignorance by knowledge will not be enough to deal with the spiritual realities and moral challenges of the future." Professor Pelikan was absolutely right: knowledge, on its own, has never been enough to deal with the moral complexities and spiritual uncertainties of our lives. Even the world's best brain surgeon cannot remove the cancer of violence from the mind of a murderer, anymore than an expert heart surgeon can remove the systemic sin of selfishness from a society that always insists on having more, more, more. There are some things in life we simply cannot learn from a lecture.

That is why the earliest laws of Harvard include knowing God as the "main end of . . . life and studies." That is why the founders of the College of William & Mary (1693) forged ahead with their vision to create "a seminary . . . of the Gospel" even when the diplomat in charge of their endowment responded to their plans by shouting, "Souls! Damn your souls! Make tobacco!" That is why the seal of Yale University (1701) is an open Bible with the words *Lux et Veritas* [Light and Truth] inscribed beneath it. And that is why ministers transformed by the Great Awakening of the eighteenth century founded Princeton (1746) with the motto *Vitam Mortuis Reddo* [I Restore Life to the Dead].

FINDING YOUR PLACE IN HISTORY

The Christian college has no need to apologize
for its existence. It was the pioneer.

—J. EDWIN ORR, *CAMPUS AFLAME*

The early stories of Harvard, William & Mary, Yale and Princeton—

and, of course, the pioneering narratives of so many other colleges and universities that followed in their wake—help us remember the surprising history of holy rebellion out of which our campuses originally emerged. Contrary to the modern trend of pitting faith and scholarship against one another, the extraordinary spiritual legacy these earliest campuses extend to us is the essential knowledge that God and academia are by no means mutually exclusive. Indeed, if Harvard's first heretic could speak to us now, he would probably encourage us toward two simple areas of application:

1. Find out more about why your campus was founded in the first place: it will help you know how to pray. A good place to start looking for that sort of information is the "About" section on most college and university websites.

2. By all means create some sacred space—whether in a dorm room, an old chapel or an unused classroom—and begin to engage with God in prayer. For thoughts on what that might look like, check out www.24-7prayer.com.

London, 1738. *Newgate was more of a dungeon than a prison, with dank and loathsome conditions, and a bloody reputation for dealing with criminals in the most expedient manner the law would allow. In eighteenth-century England, over one hundred crimes were punishable by death.*

The raw stench of open sewer forced a stifled retch from the Oxford grad as he lowered his head and crept into the uninviting darkness of the cramped cell. Because he was fasting that day, Charles Wesley had very little food in his stomach and was able to restrain his strong impulse to heave.

Wesley was not at Newgate as a criminal but rather as a visiting minister. Indeed, ever since his student days at Oxford, Charles and his brother John had taken the words of Jesus from the Gospel of Matthew literally. "I was in prison," the Gospel remembers Jesus as saying, "and you came to visit me."

The labored breathing of a black slave, trembling violently from a vicious fever and curled up in the corner of his cell like an abandoned street child on the verge of death, stirred Wesley's compassion. Having stolen from his master a month before, the slave would be hanged in a week because of his crime. Wasting away in the cruel confines of Newgate, the dark-skinned prisoner stared at the fair-skinned stranger as he entered the cell and sat down on the filthy floor beside him.

"My first year at college," Wesley confesses in his journal, "I lost in diversions." Charles's older brother John, a graduate of Oxford himself and a lecturer at Lincoln College, was very troubled by his younger brother's lack of focus. John's concern, though, must have come across a bit too forcefully at first, as Charles responded to his older brother's counsel with, "What, would you have me be a saint all at once?"

During his second year of studies, however, while his older brother was away at Epworth attending their sick father, Charles determined to take advantage of the Oxford environment. "I set myself to study," he writes in his journal, "Diligence led me into serious thinking. I went to the weekly sacrament, and persuaded two or three young students to accompany me, and to observe the method of study prescribed by the statutes of the university."

Through rhythms of prayer and open accountability with one another, this unlikely collection of Oxford lads began to intentionally give themselves and their studies to God. When John returned to the university the next year, Charles and the group, which by this point had begun to be mocked as the "Holy Club" by some other students, asked John to help them in their spiritual development.

One of the young men who joined the Wesley brothers in their early Oxford endeavor was a practically minded and keenly devoted student named William Morgan, who suggested that alongside the group's private spirituality they should begin serving others also. There were orphaned children to be educated, homeless families to be cared for, and plenty of prisoners wasting away in decrepit conditions. Thus the Holy Club, eager for God's approval, determined to alleviate such suffering as best they knew how.

The group lived by a disciplined rule of life and study that included fasting on Wednesdays and Fridays, careful accountability regarding their thoughts and actions, teaching poor families, overseeing a local school for orphans, and regularly visiting prisoners. As their devotion grew, so too did their reputation, with William Morgan's concerned father writing him from home during this period, "You cannot conceive what noise that ridiculous society which you are engaged in, has made here."

There were other observers of the Holy Club, however, who rather than mocking the group or being overly concerned about their peculiar habits, were instead drawn to them. "I had heard of, and loved them before I came to the university," a poor student named George Whitefield writes in his journal during this time, "and so strenuously defended them when I heard them reviled by students, that they be-

gan to think that I also in time should be one of them."

The Holy Club was just one of a number of demeaning titles that tagged this group during their Oxford days; they were also known as "Bible Moths" and "Enthusiasts." One label of disdain, however, outlasted all the rest. Reflecting in his journal on the curious title a number of years later, Wesley recalls it was particularly the Holy Club's rhythmical spirituality and methodical life discipline for which he and his friends were especially mocked, "This gained me the harmless name of Methodist."

The damp and rat-infested cell at Newgate seemed a long way removed from the hallowed halls of Oxford, but Charles Wesley could not help but see the similarities he shared with the sick and imprisoned slave. Only two months before the young minister had been racked by a deadly fever as well, and his emotive mind had fiercely wrestled with the enslaving fear of facing eternity without faith.

At the height of his illness, though, wearied in spirit and desperately sick in body, Wesley had finally found peace with God. "I lay musing and trembling," his journal records, with "a violent opposition and reluctance to believe, yet still the Spirit of God strove with my own and the evil spirit, till by degrees he chased away the darkness of my unbelief. I found myself convinced," Wesley confesses at last, "I knew not how, nor when, and immediately fell to prayer."

In what would become a lifelong pattern for the poetic young preacher, Wesley responded to his transforming experience through the passion of verse:

Where shall my wondering soul begin?
How shall I all to heaven aspire?
A slave redeemed from death and sin.
A brand plucked from eternal fire.

Even though the inequitable circumstances of eighteenth-century society demanded different destinies of Wesley and the slave, they were each, in the words of the young poet-preacher, equally in need of redemption "from death and sin." And on that most important count,

Wesley assured the man condemned to die, a minister was as much a "slave" to the consequences of sin as any other human. Wesley's journal offers a glimpse of the conversation they shared:

> I told him of one who came down from heaven to save lost sinners, and him in particular; described the sufferings of the Son of God, his sorrows, agony, and death. He listened with all the signs of eager astonishment; the tears trickled down his cheeks while he cried, "What! was it for me? Did God suffer all this for so poor a creature as me?"

Three days later, Wesley writes, "I preached there again with an enlarged heart; and rejoiced with my poor happy [slave]; who now believes the Son of God loved him, and gave himself for him." The young minister visited Newgate every day that week, spending time with the slave and other prisoners, encouraging them through teaching and sharing with them the bread and wine of Communion.

On the morning of the public execution, an unruly crowd, eager to witness the hangings and jostling for position, gathered in front of the gallows. Wesley arrived at the prison gates shortly before six and spent the early morning hours with the prisoners. "At half-hour past nine their irons were knocked off," he records in his journal, "and their hands tied," meaning it was time for them to be transported to the area of execution.

In a sacred act of solidarity, Wesley climbed into the execution cart to bolster the prisoners' faith as they prepared to face the mob. The sight of the young minister, side by side with the accused, created a calming effect in the crowd as the criminals' cart drew near the gallows. Looking each of the prisoners in the eye and assuring them of a faith stronger than fear, Wesley commended them to God and climbed down from the cart.

"None showed any natural terror of death: no fear, or crying, or tears," Charles Wesley records in his journal on July 19, 1738:

> All expressed their desire of our following them to paradise. I never saw such calm triumph, such incredible indifference to dying. . . . When the cart drew off, not one stirred, or struggled for

*life, but meekly gave up their spirits. . . . I spoke a few suitable words to the crowd; and returned, full of peace and confidence in our friends' happiness. That hour under the gallows was the most blessed hour of my life.**

---

*For more on the early history of Methodism, see especially the journals of John and Charles Wesley; John Whitehead's *The Life of Wesley*; Frederick C. Gill's *Charles Wesley the First Methodist*; and Harry S. Stout's *The Divine Dramatist: George Whitefield and the Rise of Modern Evangelicalism*.

HOW STUDENTS SHAPE HISTORY

OLD OXFORD'S HOLY CLUB AND NEW ENGLAND'S GREAT AWAKENING

It may be observed, the first rise of Methodism (so called) was in November 1729, when four of us met together at Oxford.

—JOHN WESLEY

History has a peculiar habit of highlighting certain people and hiding away a whole lot more. For instance, there are a few people of whom almost everyone is aware. Nelson Mandela and Billy Graham are two examples from our most recent era. George Washington and Joan of Arc, Saint Augustine and Aristotle are classic cases from more distant times. But have you ever heard of Mordecai Ham? He was the fifty-seven-year-old fiery Baptist preacher and avid supporter of the temperance movement who helped a sixteen-year-old Billy Graham decide to follow Jesus in 1934. Billy Graham has since become the most famous Protestant preacher in living history, having ministered to more than two billion people, whereas Mordecai Ham, the critical factor in Graham's conversion, has largely disappeared into the tiny footnotes of time.

As Mordecai Ham is to Billy Graham, so the Holy Club at Oxford University is to the emergence of the eighteenth-century movement called Methodism, which dramatically altered the course of Western, and in time, global history. Simple faith is sometimes followed by extraordinary results. The seemingly insignificant footnotes of history, those little-known personalities like Rev. Mordecai Ham, and, yes, those overly zealous college students like the Holy Club, are sometimes far more influential in shaping the narrative of history than we initially realize.

Now that doesn't mean such examples are perfect models we should therefore blindly emulate. Reverend Ham, for instance, although a devout minister, was well known for his holy tirades against individuals who believed (and voted) differently than he did. "If you vote for Al Smith," Ham once said of a Catholic politician running for president, "you're voting against Christ and you will all be damned." Likewise, members of the Holy Club had their own curious idiosyncrasies as well, such as John Wesley keeping his hair much longer than what was considered typical of his era.*

Regardless of the Holy Club's eccentric traits and (sometimes) excessive fasting, one area of life in which they clearly excelled was embracing the present as the essential moment that mattered most. John Gambold, a member of the earliest Oxford Methodists, remembers this trait especially at work in John Wesley: "He had neither the presumption, nor the leisure to anticipate things whose season were not now," writes Gambold in a letter in 1737, "and would show some uneasiness whenever any of us . . . were shifting off the appointed improvement of the present minute."

One of the greatest myths and most disempowering concepts of our collegiate years is the faulty idea that *real life starts later*. As if the daily decisions that deeply influence our friends, significantly shape our campuses and regularly recenter our lives have no actual bearing in *the real world*. Had the Holy Club bought into that bogus belief, the world they would eventually transform might still be waiting for some humble and courageous souls to take the risk of actually *doing something* in the present, rather than forever waiting for the idyllic environment of the future (where apparently *the real world*—that mythical

---

*For the record, John Wesley claimed that by not cutting his hair he was able to save more money for the poor, and—who knows?—he may have also just liked having long hair.

place where all your decisions really *do* matter—is eagerly lying in wait).

THE (MIS)EDUCATION OF THE HOLY CLUB AND THE MOVEMENT THEY HELPED INSPIRE

Their undertaking included these several particulars . . .
to visit the prisons, to instruct some poor families, to
take care of a school and a parish workhouse. They [also]
took great pains with the younger members of the
university, to rescue them from bad company, and
encourage them in a sober, studious life. They would get
them to breakfast, and over a dish of tea endeavor to
fashion some good hint upon them.

—JOHN GAMBOLD

Edward Gibbon, author of the eighteenth-century classic *The Rise and Fall of the Roman Empire*, was a contemporary of the Wesley brothers and studied at Oxford shortly after they did. Gibbon's recollections of his time at Oxford, a period he describes in his *Memoirs* as "the most idle and unprofitable of my whole life," reveals a characteristic far too common of students in general: *boredom*. The Oxford Methodists intentionally countered such dullness by applying their hearts and hands, their minds and talents, to the pressing issues of their age. If Gibbon's assessment was accurate and the university system of that era lacked in purposeful education at times, the Wesley brothers and their Holy Club sparked a counterculture of *miseducation* that was decidedly intentional in its disciplined engagement with both life and learning.*

---

*Now, that doesn't mean the Holy Club was necessarily a group of avid scholars renowned for their diligent study habits. For example, George Whitefield, according to Harry Stout in *The Divine Dramatist*, "remained indifferent . . . to classical learning and sustained study" throughout his entire life. The point is not that they were perfect students but that they applied themselves to life and learning in a *countercultural* and *intentional* way.

"Their main singularity," writes Frederick Gill in *Charles Wesley the First Methodist,* "was that they were out of tune with contemporary cynicism and indifference." Such a shift was desperately needed, especially considering the dire circumstances of England during this time. Massive population growth meant there were more mouths to feed and fierce competition for the few jobs to be had. Added to this predicament of widespread unemployment and fermenting public frustration was an epidemic of alcoholism. Of 2,000 houses in one district of London in 1750, 506 of them were gin shops. Poverty and alcohol addiction are a bad combination at any time, but particularly when partnered with the social upheaval of the Enlightenment, the bloody profiteering of the British slave trade and the urban breakdown that accompanied the dawn of the Industrial Revolution. Eighteenth century England was in a real mess.

Taking into account the dangerously unstable situation, perhaps it is not so surprising that legal courts of that era determined more than one hundred crimes were deserving of death; the judges probably thought it was the only way to keep the peace. Imagine then, in that rough and volatile setting, the reviving effect in society when some devoted students from Oxford begin to practically engage with the immense social challenges that were threatening full-scale revolution in England. The Holy Club was certainly not the only group of its kind at work in the British Isles, but with the steady emergence of the movement called Methodism, it was surely the most lasting.

Although the Wesley brothers and their friends were eager to stay at Oxford and continue their work there, the group slowly began to disperse after John and Charles left the university and made their way as missionaries to the American colony of Georgia in 1735. Their post in the New World was only shortly served, however, with each of them meeting great discouragement in their failed mission endeavors. "I went to America, to convert the Indians," John confesses in his journal in 1738, "but who shall convert me?"

Sometimes, though, as the life of John Wesley so clearly demonstrates, through failure we find what we are looking for all along. For soon after John returned in defeat to England, he experienced a transformative moment of trusting in God that redirected his life calling and empowered the emerging movement he would soon be leading. "I felt my heart strangely warmed," Wesley writes of the moment in his journal on May 24, 1738, "I felt I did trust in Christ, Christ alone for my salvation."

John's younger brother Charles and his dear friend from Oxford, George Whitefield, had recently experienced a similar sort of conversion as well. When Whitefield decided to take his message of faith to the fields, because the established churches were increasingly concerned about the enthusiasm that marked his stirring sermons, the size of Whitefield's audiences grew from hundreds to thousands. Although John Wesley would effectively channel this surge of Jesus interest into lasting discipleship, George Whitefield was the activating voice of the movement.

GEORGE WHITEFIELD AND THE GREAT AWAKENING

I hardly ever knew him go through a sermon
without weeping, [and] I truly believe his were
the tears of sincerity.

—CORNELIUS WINTER,
COMMENTING ON GEORGE WHITEFIELD

Studying at Oxford may not have transformed George Whitefield into a renowned scholar, but it did prompt him toward a surprising new depth in his spirituality. Unlike most others students, Whitefield was admitted to Oxford as a *servitor*, a poor student who earned his way through university by serving the wealthier scholars. When he was not at work or studying, he mostly kept to himself and quickly became, according to his own admission, a lonely *odd fellow* obsessed with prayers and fasting and religious services.

During this time, Charles Wesley noticed the earnest, young student and invited him to join the Holy Club. Whitefield immediately felt at home with the group and before long was attempting to outdo the Wesley's in his reckless pursuit of God. His extreme fasting and other forms of spiritual and physical deprivation (which unfortunately left him frostbitten on one occasion) meant that Whitefield began skipping classes and not completing assignments. When confronted by his tutor about his strange behavior and how it was affecting his health and studies, Whitefield suffered a nervous breakdown and was forced to take a leave of absence from Oxford.

During his time away from university and at the peak of his soul-searching depression, George Whitefield experienced what he could only describe as a *new birth*, a spiritual conversion that finally set him free from the overwhelming religious obligations he had once felt. He returned to Oxford a different student, soon completed his course of studies and then started a remarkable ministry of preaching that made him famous in England and carried him across the Atlantic as well. In America, Whitefield became something of a national phenomenon, preaching to crowds as large as twenty and thirty thousand, the largest public gatherings the New World had ever seen.*

While there were many in the New World who eagerly welcomed Whitefield and his message, there were others who accused him of manipulating the emotions of his listeners with his dramatic flair for preaching. His sermons were unlike anything people had ever seen or heard before from a minister. Whitefield laughed and wept while he preached, issuing passionate pleas for conversion with the white-knuckled intensity of a man whose very words seemed to bridge heaven and earth. His startling style, though controversial, was extraordinarily effective and helped fan into flame a fiery era of spiritual transformation known as the Great Awakening.

The "intellectual leader" of the New England edge of this awakening was Massachusetts minister Jonathan Edwards, a brilliant thinker who entered Yale shortly before he was thirteen and graduated valedictorian four years later. Even though Edwards worked tirelessly to thoughtfully articulate the "saving affections and experiences" nec-

---

*I use the word *national* intentionally here because the itinerant preaching of Whitefield was one of the early unifying forces that enabled the American colonies to see themselves as one. Truly he was, in the insightful words of Harry Stout, the original "American Icon."

essary to genuine faith, there were many ministers who viewed the awakening as little more than a misleading and dangerous display of emotion. As a result, a fierce divide soon developed between the "New Lights" of the awakening and the established "Old Lights" of steady institutions like Harvard and Yale.

Activist leaders of the awakening, having been shut out of Harvard and Yale, thus began pioneering other colleges instead. Revivalist Presbyterians founded Princeton in 1746 and the Baptists launched Brown in 1764. Dutch Reformed clerics started Rutgers in 1766 and awakened Congregationalists founded Dartmouth in 1769. Not to be outdone by the new boys, though, Anglican leaders of the Old School started Columbia in 1754. During this time the University of Pennsylvania was also chartered through the influence of Benjamin Franklin in 1755, a colonial college considered neither New Light nor Old Light, although its first meeting house, mind you, was a structure originally built for the congregation of Ben Franklin's dear friend George Whitefield.*

The Great Awakening, even with its tremendous power, did not last long. Similar to that fabled flash of lightening that struck Ben Franklin's kite and taught him a thing or two about electricity, the electrifying awakening seemed to fade just as quickly as it had come. We will consider some of the potential reasons for the short life of America's Great Awakening in chapter three. Before we close this chapter, though, we must first return to England and briefly explore the emerging Methodist movement that was not only growing wide but decidedly deep as well.

SOCIAL HOLINESS AND THE ABOLITION OF THE BRITISH SLAVE TRADE

The Gospel of Christ knows no religion but social;
no holiness, but social holiness.

—JOHN WESLEY

---

*"I knew him intimately upwards of thirty years," Franklin said of his old friend Whitefield. "His integrity, disinterestedness and indefatigable zeal in prosecuting every good work I have never seen equaled and shall never see excelled." A statue of Whitefield adorns the campus of Penn to this day.

A rhythm of practical discipleship and steady engagement with suffering people was not simply characteristic of the Oxford Methodists: it was their DNA. Open accountability and straightforward encouragement was the Wesleyan way of dealing with personal sin. Sacrificial service to prisoners and the poor, combined with lifestyles of intentional simplicity that enabled generosity, was the early Methodist measure of genuine Christianity. Even though the Wesley brothers, after their own conversion experiences, always insisted on *faith in Jesus* as the only true way of finding acceptance with God, they equally expected such faith to be practically worked out in small-group discipleship and consistent service to others.

Early in the Methodist movement, John Wesley began gathering believers into little collectives of discipleship called societies. "Christianity is essentially a social religion," Wesley taught, "and to turn it into a solitary religion is indeed to destroy it." The societies were greenhouses for growth, providing intentional friendships of faith for new converts and also engaging believers in practical service through health care initiatives, homes for widows, schools for orphaned children and small financial loans for impoverished families. "The movement," explains Howard Snyder in *The Radical Wesley*, "was in fact a whole series of sporadic and often geographically localised [movements], which were interconnected and spread by the society . . . network."

Remarkably, even though Methodism only reached 1 percent of England's population during John Wesley's lifetime, about one hundred years after he died there were more than forty million Methodists worldwide. There were obvious weaknesses at work in a movement so large, especially evident in Wesley's early tendency toward trying to *fix* problems in society rather than *prevent* them. Simultaneously, though, weaknesses taken into account, the eighteenth-century Wesleyan movement was nevertheless an essential cultural force in affecting lasting change in society.

Undoubtedly the most noteworthy area of social transformation had to do with the British slave trade. In 1774, at the height of slavery's economic power, John Wesley wrote a booklet called *Thoughts on Slavery* and became the first leading figure in English society to openly confront the institution. Because of his convictions, slaveholders could not become full members of Methodist societies while Wesley was alive. Notably, the last letter John Wesley wrote was to a young parliamentarian named William Wilberforce, an influential figure in society who eventually led the way in abolishing the British slave trade in 1807 and the institution of British slavery as a whole in 1833.

Dubbed the "Evangelical Centaur," John Wesley was a disciple-making machine. He crisscrossed England in a flurry of service, travelling over 250,000 miles on horseback, preaching 40,000 sermons and writing approximately 250 books and tracts. His brother Charles, ever the evangelist as well, was especially well known for communicating profound depths of theology through his more than 9,000 hymns.* While it may be a bit of a stretch to say that Methodism *alone* saved eighteenth-century England from revolution, it is plainly evident that Methodism helped shape history for the better during a very volatile period of time.

One final thought to keep in mind about the Holy Club at Oxford, the Great Awakening in the New World and the Methodist movement in England is the enduring friendship the Wesley brothers and George Whitefield shared. Later in their lives they strongly disagreed with each other on certain points of theology (theirs was the classic Arminianism-Calvinism debate), but they still maintained a genuine lifelong friendship, even though it was clearly challenging at times. When George Whitefield died in 1769, John Wesley delivered the sermon at his funeral in London. The Holy Club was not only outstanding for how it helped to shape history; it was also outstanding for the lasting friendships it formed.

FINDING YOUR PLACE IN HISTORY

It was not the economists who liberated the slaves or who passed the factory acts, but the rash and ignorant Christians.

—KENNETH E. BOULDING

---

*"Why should the devil have all the good music?" Charles Wesley was known to say before borrowing the melodies of popular pub tunes and rewriting their lyrics.

Even though John Wesley is considered the father of Methodism and George Whitefield is remembered as one of the most electrifying preachers to have ever lived, it was actually Charles Wesley—a marginal student at Oxford who decided to intentionally engage with God and others—who started the Holy Club. How very different the world may be had Charles determined to *just float through his college career* instead. The turning points of history are surprisingly simple sometimes. You and I may or may not be called to lead a movement as the Wesley brothers and Whitefield did, but we do have a part to play. Here are two simple things—*guiding traits of the Holy Club*, let's call them—that will enable us to begin engaging with God and others in a more intentional way:

1. Look around you. Wherever you are right now is *the real world*. If you are not acting on what you believe in the present, then what's to say you will in the future? Shaping history is not a spectator sport.

2. Intentional friendships that include honest conversations, steady rhythms of prayer and practical service to others are essential for healthy spiritual growth. Find your collective—*create one if you must*—and explore new depths of friendship in God.

3

Princeton, 1802. *The unmistakable smell of smoke could have been caused by all manner of harmless things. An overcooked meal. A farmer clearing his land. A chimney needing to be cleaned.*

Smoke was a common smell in those days and not usually a cause for great concern. This particular day was different, however. It was March 6, and Nassau Hall was burning, but no one knew.

The one o'clock bell rang for lunch, and students and faculty were gathering in the dining room when shouts of Fire! began to echo through the old building. George Strawbridge, a senior, bolted for the doors and joined a group of fellow students outside who were standing on the campus lawn, staring in shock at the flickering flames dancing deliberately across the roof of the great hall.

Strawbridge ran back inside. Racing up the stairs to his room on the top floor, he grabbed his water jug and began dousing the burning door that led to the bell tower. The president of the college, Samuel Stanhope Smith, burst into the room behind Strawbridge in an attempt to help the student contain the fire.

It was too late. An unforgiving southwest wind had already provided the rooftop fire with all the force and oxygen it needed to transform itself from a few small flames into an unrelenting blaze. Assessing the situation and realizing the flames were out of control, President Smith raised his hands in desperation and cried aloud, "This is the progress of vice and irreligion!"

There were numerous attempts to extinguish the fire that day, but the furious burning proved unbeatable. As the conflagration consumed the roof, students and staff salvaged all they could from the floors beneath, piling books and furniture, personal clothes and rare science equipment into a heaping mass on the campus lawn.

When the roof of the college finally caved in, only one hundred volumes of the more than three thousand books in the library were saved.

Everything else was destroyed. Almost fifty years in the making, the historic Nassau Hall was now in ashes, with blackened passageways and empty classrooms reduced to smoking frames.

President Smith was convinced, as were a committee of investigating trustees, that renegade students had deliberately set the college ablaze. The fire was an "effect of those irreligious & demoralizing principles," wrote Stanhope Smith in an 1802 letter to a colleague in Boston, "which are tearing the bands of society asunder & threatening in the end to overturn our country." The dangerous "principles" to which Smith was referring were stirrings of religious and social dissent, particularly among young people, fanned into flame after the American Revolution through French philosophers like Voltaire and "irreligious" writings like Tom Paine's Age of Reason.

Young Strawbridge, in contrast to the conclusion of the president and trustees, was not convinced the fire was as sinister as the overseers assumed, in time referring to their indictment as "the weakest charge of incendiarism I have ever heard." Whether the fire was intentionally set or simply the result of negligence, history does not reveal.

Regardless, however, President Smith and the trustees immediately invested themselves in the purposeful work of rebuilding Nassau Hall and again laying claim to the original design of the college. In fact, only a few weeks after the devastating fire, the renovations and fundraising began in earnest. By August 1802, less than six months later, the report went out that "Nassau Hall is rebuilding with great speed."

During the ensuing years a steady influx of students, partially the result of a good reputation gained from the quick and admirable rebuilding after the fire, meant the new Nassau Hall was soon packed with too many scholars and not enough professors. Even though President Smith was pursuing a solid path of education that sought to blend modern advances in science with a scholarly understanding of faith, the pressures of overpopulated classrooms and underdeveloped tutors soon resulted in dire consequences.

A series of disciplinarian problems—including a drunk senior creat-

ing havoc in town, a tutor cursed for trying to quell a disturbance in a junior's dorm room and a sophomore smuggling "strong liquor into the college"—led to a very volatile gathering of students and staff in the main meeting room of Nassau Hall on April 1, 1807.

The evening meeting was meant to deal with what the president and trustees viewed as a mounting movement toward anarchy at the college. But when an influential student on campus rose to his feet shouting, most of the student body joined the young revolutionary in open rebellion and burst out of the building, according to one nineteenth-century observer, "like drunken Indians."

Windows were shattered and doors were broken as the student riot turned violent and the local militia was summoned to regain control of the campus. The young rebels, inspired in their cause by the revolutionary spirit of their newly independent nation, gathered clubs and rocks as weapons and barricaded the doors of Nassau Hall, defiantly daring anyone to enter. The college was closed the next day.

Although Nassau Hall reopened a month after the rebellion, the disastrous riot of 1807 contributed to a significant shift in direction for Princeton. In actuality, even before the fire of 1802, which was supposedly set by disgruntled and revolutionary students, there had been murmurings of the need for another institution to be established—a theological seminary of sorts—set apart for the serious training of young ministers.

The evident weakening in religious values at the college and a steady decline of ministerial graduates resulted in Princeton's Theological Seminary being founded in 1812. It was also the year that Samuel Stanhope Smith stepped down from his position as president, as the trustees were increasingly wary of his educational ideas that merged historical Christianity with the new science of reason.

The birth of the seminary and the departure of Stanhope Smith meant certain reform for the college at Princeton. Under the leadership of the newly appointed president, Ashbel Green, the college was to enter a period of spiritual renewal, a return to its original design, as it were. The students, however, had a different agenda in mind.

On January 9, 1814, a hollow log was packed with two pounds of gunpowder and set against one of the back doors of Nassau Hall. When the contraption detonated, it blew apart the doors, shattered panes of window glass throughout the building and propelled a large piece of the log through the door of the Prayer Hall. Even though the perpetrators were caught and tried, it did not deter other riotous students from similar actions, including a pistol being fired outside a tutor's door four months later.

By November 1814 the spiritual atmosphere began to shift. A small collection of praying students, influenced by awakenings at Yale and a few other colleges, helped to turn the tide on the campus at Princeton. "The divine influence," wrote President Green, "seemed to descend like the silent dew of heaven and in about four weeks there were few individuals in the college edifice who were not deeply impressed with a sense of the importance of spiritual and eternal things."

Before long, the same students who were planning to burn down outhouses and plotting classroom revolts were gathering their friends for prayer instead. It was as if the spiritual consciousness of the college, lulled to sleep by the intoxicating questions of the age of reason, was suddenly awakened to the reality of God. "It was a period," records Green in an 1815 report on the revival, "never to be forgotten by those who witnessed its remarkable impressions and transformations."

Sustained by a weekly prayer gathering, the awakening lasted throughout a large portion of 1815 and into early parts of 1816 as well. By January 1817, however, the familiar spirit of student discontent had returned, and this time with a vengeance. The consequent riot, which included armed violence, resulted in seven arrests and twenty-four students being dismissed from the college.*

---

*For more on this period of Princeton's history, see Thomas J. Wertenbaker, *Princeton: 1746–1896;* Mark A. Noll, *Princeton and the Republic, 1768–1822: The Search for a Christian Enlightenment in the Era of Samuel Stanhope Smith;* and Frederick Rudolph, "Legacy of the Revolution," in *The American College and University: A History.*

RIOTS AND REVIVAL AT PRINCETON

THE CURIOUS CASE OF THE MODERN MIND

Have you heard the terrible news from Princeton?

—REV. SAMUEL MILLER,
COMMENTING ON THE 1807 RIOTS

The era that followed the American Revolution was a grand and risky experiment in independent thinking and representative government. British oversight had successfully been ousted from the colonies, and irreligious strains of French philosophy were rapidly gaining traction on college campuses. As a result, authority in general—in church and state, on campus and in society—was increasingly up for grabs. The effect on students, as evidenced by the 1807 and 1817 riots at Nassau Hall, was extraordinary.

Princeton, mind you, was certainly not alone in its experience of campus upheaval. The typical student at Harvard in the "early seventeen-nineties was an atheist in religion, an experimentalist in morals, a rebel in authority," writes Samuel Morison in *Three Centuries of Harvard.* In two other telling cases of postrevolutionary campus mayhem, an antichurch play was performed at Dartmouth and a mock communion service was celebrated at Williams. Perhaps it should not have been so surprising, then, when the dean of Princeton opened the Prayer Hall Bible in 1813 and out fell a pack of playing cards.

These episodes of social and religious revolt are particularly important because of how this dynamic period of postrevolutionary history affected the overall spiritual life out of which America's earliest colleges emerged. Especially significant at Princeton, for example, was the founding of the theological seminary in 1812 as a separate institution from the college. The reason for the divide between college and seminary seemed fairly straightforward at the time. The church needed more leaders, and the college, with its students struggling through fires and riots and rebellions, was simply not producing enough ministers. The newly founded seminary, therefore, would solely give itself to the serious training of church leaders.*

What made the campus divide between college and seminary more complicated than it originally seemed, however, is the subtle but significant distance it created between serious studies about God and serious studies about the rest of life. That divide, very specifically, is *the curious case of the modern mind:* an intellectual split between sacred and secular learning. With the emergence of the seminary, the college was no longer the central environment for the focused development of faith it once was. In that regard, the seminary had taken precedence.

In some ways it is important that such a shift took place. "Christianity, whatever else it is," George Marsden reminds us in *The Secularization of the Academy,* "is not the same as American culture, and hence it cannot be co-extensive with its public institutions." (The early colleges were of course private, but the broader point of confusing American culture with Christian faith still applies.) Freedom of religion in America means the education system in America must not be controlled by a prevailing religious mindset.

Simultaneously, though, as education continued to evolve in the United States, the increasing distance between "holy" and "worldly" learning resulted in a confusing divide between heart and head in our overall view of life. In time, Bible colleges would represent one end of the spectrum and decidedly secular research universities would rep-

---

*With similar motivations in mind, Andover Seminary was founded in 1808 as a response to discouraging theological trends at Harvard, and a separate seminary at Yale would eventually follow suit in 1822.

resent the other. Before we consider the wider implications of that divide, and especially how it has influenced our understanding of repentance, we must first revisit the spiritual legacy left to us by the Great Awakening.

LOOKING BACK AT THE GREAT AWAKENING

The revivals of the 1730s and 1740s did produce a dramatic interest in religion, to which numerous observers attest. Yet after the fires of revival cooled, membership additions dipped below earlier averages, and by the 1750s many churches that had benefited from the revivals were barely adding enough new members to replace those who died.

—MARK NOLL

One of the most important questions we must ask about the Great Awakening, that lightning-like revival that lit-up New England and ignited spiritual life throughout the colonies in the eighteenth century, is, Where did all that energy go? According to the *Encyclopedia of Religious Revivals in America*, the Great Awakening was experienced in thirty-four towns in Massachusetts, nine communities in Connecticut, and twenty-five settlements across New Jersey and Pennsylvania. Even Ben Franklin, an open skeptic of such movements, was struck by the revival's remarkable influence. "Never did the people show so great a willingness to attend sermons," Franklin wrote in the *Pennsylvania Gazette* on June 12, 1740. "No books are in request but those of piety."

The vital strength of the awakening, and one of the reasons it grew so quickly, was its profound accessibility. George Whitefield, for example, preached in such a way as to make the gospel relevant to the lives and experiences of coal miners and slaves. The Great Awakening was certainly not a movement limited to scholars and professors, and neither should it have been. For when Jesus chose his unlikely collection of disciples in the first place, he gave the keys of his kingdom to very "ordinary" people.*

Surely it was with this sort of perspective in mind that influential leaders of the trans-Atlantic awakening sought to make the revival a movement for common people. In fact, that is probably one of the reasons why George Whitefield preferred to preach in open fields and community gathering grounds (like Boston Common) instead of exclusively preaching in church buildings. It is also why John Wesley, in a very controversial move in England, began to ordain lay preachers—Methodist men and women not professionally trained at university, but clearly displaying *an understanding of the Bible* and *a personal experience of salvation*—as ministers of the gospel.

The vital benefit of this sort of transformation, from the traditional norms of religious practice to the dynamic innovations of revival, is that it enabled a very unpretentious and down-to-earth faith. Preaching without notes and spontaneous prayer, both occasional hallmarks of the awakening, resulted in a deeper emotional connection to God. Where religious doctrines had become increasingly dry, the anointed words of revivalists fell like rain. Religion was no longer limited to the bounds of one's *intellect*; faith was now something to be experienced in one's *heart* as well.

The essential takeaway of this extraordinary period was a new and dynamic understanding of faith. It was a *thoughtful faith* that deeply valued intellectual knowledge about God, as evidenced in the founding of Princeton, Brown, Rutgers and Dartmouth. But it was also a *faith of profound feeling* that equally valued a living experience of God, as evidenced by the powerful displays of emotion that commonly accompanied revival preaching throughout this time. Striking the delicate balance between heart and head is never easy, though, is it?

---

*According to the book of Acts, this is one of the reasons the earliest followers of Jesus created such a stir: "When [the religious leaders] saw the courage of Peter and John and realized that they were unschooled, ordinary men, they were astonished and they took note that these men had been with Jesus" (Acts 4:13 TNIV).

HEART AND HEAD: BRIDGING THE GREAT DIVIDE

The majority of revivalists undoubtedly preferred a nice
balance between intellect and emotion, but as itinerants
and exhorters quickened the tempo, their emphasis fell
less on learning and more on the heart and its needs.

—DAVID S. LOVEJOY

Because the Great Awakening was marked by such intense emotion, which included people crying out in the middle of messages and sometimes falling from their pews as if struck by invisible power, the revival resulted in a fundamental rethinking of what it actually meant to be a Christian. As to whether or not knowing God was essentially a matter of heart or head, extreme positions emerged on both sides. For example, a traveling preacher named James Davenport, especially well known for his stirring enthusiasm, went so far as to publicly burn the books of the more traditionally inclined ministers with whom he disagreed.*

As a result of this growing tension between the emotions and the mind, the distance between heart and head Christianity became increasingly evident. The dividing wedge would grow even greater during the natural versus supernatural debate of the Enlightenment. Our split spirituality would be taken a step further still with the campus divide between college and seminary that occurred soon after that. To this very day, in fact, we continue to struggle with the daunting spiritual tension that seems to separate the saving of our souls and the saving of our minds.

One of the striking results of this tension, and vitally important as it relates to the central message of this book, is what might be called the *revival-fix-all mentality.* This is a way of thinking (and praying) that views spiritual awakening as a one-shot silver bullet that will effectively and finally deal with the critical issues of our age. When we apply that theory to the Great Awakening, however, what we discover is

---

*Davenport then decided to make a most memorable point by tossing his trousers into the same fire. I've yet to discover what his precise point was.

very surprising. The period immediately after the revival (from about 1750 to 1790) was marked by a serious decline in active faith, rather than a substantial increase.

While the immediate effect of the awakening was clearly astonishing, one of the real weaknesses of this period in U.S. history is that many influential Christian leaders were not at the forefront of reshaping public opinion as it related to two of the most significant social sins of the day, the unjust treatment of Native Americans and the forced enslavement of Africans. In 1845, a full century after the Great Awakening, the former slave Frederick Douglass wrote,

> Between the Christianity of this land, and the Christianity of Christ, I recognize the widest possible difference. . . .
>
> I love the pure . . . and impartial Christianity of Christ; I therefore hate the corrupt, slaveholding, women-whipping, cradle-plundering, partial and hypocritical Christianity of this land. Indeed, I can see no reason, but the most deceitful one, for calling the religion of this land Christianity.

When the full-bodied message of Jesus is reduced to the *saving of souls* alone, we fail in our equally essential calling of exercising the *mind of Christ* in working toward creative and thoughtful solutions for the pressing issues of our age. Learning to think like Jesus is a vital part of learning to live like Jesus. "Let each of you look not only to your own interests," the apostle Paul wrote in the letter to the Philippians, "but also to the interest of others. Have this *mind* among yourselves, which is yours in Christ Jesus" (Philippians 2:4-11 ESV, italics added).

It is popular in some circles to shut down the intellect because of a concern that it will only distract from the deeper things of the spirit. Such ideas are often based on a misunderstanding of a portion of 1 Corinthians that reads: "God chose what is foolish in this world to shame the wise" (1 Corinthians 1:27 ESV). The main point of this passage is not to discourage us from deep thinking, however, but to keep us mindful of the humility of the cross. In actual fact, the biblical idea of repentance begins with a deep and thorough rethinking of every aspect of our lives.

CHANGING OUR MINDS ABOUT REPENTANCE

The problem is not only to win souls but to save minds.
If you win the whole world and lose the mind of
the world, you will soon discover you have not won the
world. Indeed it may turn out that you have actually
lost the world.

—CHARLES MALIK

There is more to repentance than feeling really sorry about our sins, having an authentic experience with God or creating a theological contract with Jesus to be certain our souls will be welcomed into heaven when the time comes. *Repentance* is a much more loaded word than that. It actually comes from the Greek word *metanoia*, which is made up of two parts: *meta* means "change" and *noia* means "mind." Thus *repentance* has a whole lot to do with *changing our minds*.

Knowledge, it must be understood, is never evil in and of itself, and neither is it necessarily good, for that matter. God's original warning against eating from "the tree of the knowledge of good and evil" had less to do with our heads and more to do with our hearts. The essential problem of sin is not that humans would develop the brainpower to split an atom, but that we would not have the heart power to keep ourselves from using the atom bomb. Foreseeing centuries of violence and the bloody cycle of sin that perpetuates suffering, God warned us, "If you eat its fruit, you are sure to die" (Genesis 2:16-17).

Is it possible the Creator would have eventually welcomed Adam and Eve to partake of the fruit of knowledge once they had grown into a mature and trusting relationship with God, in the same way a loving parent eventually teaches a child the benefits of fire after the little one has learned not to touch an open flame? Perhaps. Either way, though, the Bible is abundantly clear that the Creator is certainly not opposed to knowledge in general, as elsewhere in Scripture God mourns for a people who are "destroyed for a lack of knowledge" (Hosea 4:6 ESV) and the ancient prophets dream of a day when

the earth will be filled
with the knowledge of the glory of the LORD
as the waters cover the sea. (Habakkuk 2:14 ESV)

The problem is not the extraordinary potential of the human mind but the astonishing pride of the human heart. Truly we are like children playing with fire. Through the humility of repentance, however, Jesus not only offers us salvation from the fiery consequences of our arrogance, he also empowers us to "be transformed," in the words of Romans, "by the renewing of [our] mind" (Romans 12:2 NIV).

An exceptional example of the power of repentance took place at Yale during the same time frame as the cycles of riots and revival at Princeton. When Timothy Dwight, the grandson of Jonathan Edwards, accepted the presidency of Yale in 1795, he invited the students into an open debate regarding the truth of the Scriptures. Rather than staying silent about the irreligious philosophies of the time, which the previous administration had chosen to do, Dwight decided to address the genuine intellectual concerns of his students in a series of remarkable chapel messages. "For the next six months," explains Charles Cuningham in a biography about Dwight, "he preached steadily on the subject. As far as he was concerned, the more discussion there was, the better."

During the next few years, Dwight continued to gain ground at Yale, and in 1802 the campus experienced a profound spiritual awakening that resulted in one third of the student body deciding to follow Jesus. As the Yale awakening multiplied to other campuses, the most notable transformation in the widespread student revival was of the *mind*. "There was undoubtedly an appeal to the hearts of the students," writes J. Edwin Orr in *Campus Aflame*, "but . . . their minds and consciences were moved [too]."

When talking of, praying for and working toward transformation on campuses, we must not dilute the full-orbed revolutionary message of heart *and* head repentance. God does not intend to suppress our minds in order to awaken our souls. That sort of thinking (or perhaps lack of it) is more likely to lead to cycles of riots and revival than to lasting transformation. The extraordinary challenges of our time demand extraordinarily wise and creative solutions. Our minds, humbled through repentance and empowered by the Holy Spirit, must become more engaged than ever before.

FINDING YOUR PLACE IN HISTORY

It has always been a sin not to love the Lord our God with our minds as well as our hearts and souls. . . . We have excused this with a degree of pietism and pretend[ing] that this is something other than what it is—that is, sin.

—OS GUINNESS

The urgent need of our generation, and one of the most important themes of this book, is the rejoining of heart and head in our understanding of spiritual awakening and especially in our day-to-day following of Jesus. Even though the curious case of the modern mind drove a dividing wedge between the sacred and the secular, one of the redemptive elements of the postmodern mind is a genuine desire to bridge that great divide. Can you imagine the global effect in communications and the arts, in the fields of business and science and technology, and in education and healthcare and diplomacy if a new breed of believers emerged on campus whose entire lives (heart, soul, mind and strength) were fully surrendered to Jesus?

1. *Change your mind* about what it means to follow Jesus. Salvation is much more than we have made it. When you invited Jesus into your heart, did you invite him into your mind too?

2. *Change your expectations* about revival. The goal is not simply an exciting spiritual experience. (Although such times will probably come too!) The goal is Christ-centered, Spirit-empowered, compassionate people of faith sacrificially living like Jesus in every area of culture and society.

INTERLUDE

Reflections on Campus Foundations

What else can save us but your hand

remaking what you have made?

—SAINT AUGUSTINE

Foundations matter. When it comes to a building, the strength or weakness of the foundations determines how long the structure will stand. When it comes to a story, the foundations of the story—the introduction of style and critical characters, place and period—most often reveal the general direction the narrative will take. When it comes to colleges and universities, it is the foundations of such institutions that help us understand *why they were founded in the first place* and *what the point is of praying for them right now*. Foundations matter.

Before the signing of the Declaration of Independence in 1776, there were nine officially chartered colleges in the colonies. Although I have already mentioned each of these campuses, it is helpful to see them as a complete group: Harvard, William & Mary, Yale, Princeton, Columbia, Penn, Brown, Rutgers and Dartmouth. Commonly called the *colonial colleges*, these nine pioneering institutions represent the earliest foundations of Campus America.

While each of the colonial colleges has its own unique history, common to all of them is a *foundation of faith*. Their earliest stories reveal they were founded either as an impulse of New England Puritanism, as a revived form of Anglicanism or as a dynamic outgrowth of the Great Awakening. Their mottoes demonstrate the original design of the colonial colleges and offer an important reminder of why collegiate communities in America were created in the first place:

Harvard (1636)
> *Veritas* and *Christo et Ecclesiae*
> "Truth" and "For Christ and the Church"

Yale (1701)
> *Lux et Veritas*
> "Light and Truth"

Princeton (1746)
> *Vitam Mortuis Reddo* and *Dei Sub Numine Viget*
> "I restore life to the dead" and "Under God's power she
> flourishes"

Penn (1740/1755)
> *Leges Sine Moribus Vanae*
> "Laws without morals are in vain"

Columbia (1754)
> *In Lumine Tuo Videbimus Lumen*
> "In Thy light shall we see light" (Psalm 36:9)

Brown (1764)
> *In Deo Speramus*
> "In God we hope"

Rutgers (1766)
> *Sol Iustitiae et Occidentem Illustra*
> "Sun of righteousness, shine upon the West also"

Dartmouth (1769)
> *Vox Clamantis in Deserto*
> "A voice crying out in the wilderness" (Matthew 3:3)[*]

---

*The College of William & Mary (1693) is not included in this list because it does not have a motto.

Only the University of Pennsylvania might stand distinct from this lineage of faith, but that depends on when you date Penn's founding. As previously mentioned, the University of Pennsylvania was officially chartered through the influence of Ben Franklin in 1755, but Penn prefers to trace its origin to a charity school inspired by George Whitefield and originally proposed in 1740. The preference for the earlier date is because 1740 positions Penn as the fourth oldest of the colonial colleges. If Penn's preference for the 1740 date is honored, then there is clearly no denying that all nine of the colonial colleges were specifically founded with faith in mind.*

Alongside the colonial colleges a few other schools were founded during the colonial era but were not officially chartered as colleges until after America gained independence. The earliest stories of these schools reveal a striking legacy of faith as well. For example, Moravian College in Bethlehem, Pennsylvania, traces its roots to a school started in 1742 by sixteen-year-old Countess Benigna von Zinzendorf. Benigna was the daughter of Count Nicholas von Zinzendorf, the leader of a Moravian faith community in Europe who created a 24/7 prayer chain that lasted over one hundred years and helped launch the modern missions movement.

Dickinson College was established as a grammar school in 1773 and chartered as a college in 1778, only five days after the American Revolutionary War ended. Its original seal, which Dickinson uses to this day, displays a liberty cap, a telescope and an open Bible. Hampden-Sydney College, located in Virginia, was started in 1775 and officially chartered in 1783. Its Greek motto, *Gnosesthe ten Aletheian*, comes from the Gospel of John and is translated, "You will know the truth."

The sacred and ancient legacy of Jesus-centered education extends much further back than the colonial colleges of America and has in fact vitally influenced the development of education around the

---

*Whether you think the University of Pennsylvania was founded in 1740 or 1755, what is especially unique to Penn's pioneering reforms in education is that unlike other colonial colleges, it did not mainly focus on the training of ministers but instead prepared students for service in multiple spheres of society.

world. The University of Freiburg, for instance, established in Germany in 1457 and considered one of the top-ranking universities in Europe today, was founded with the motto, *Die Wahrheit wird euch frei machen*, "The truth will make you free." Similar to Hampden-Sydney, the University of Freiburg's motto is based on Jesus' words in the Gospel of John.

The oldest university in the English-speaking world is Oxford, whose history of teaching extends all the way back to 1096. Oxford's motto, *Dominus Illuminatio Mea*, comes from Psalm 27 and is translated, "The Lord is my light." Although a comprehensive study of the original stories behind colleges and universities around the world has yet to be done, it is obvious that God and campus have been in vital partnership from the very beginning.

That foundational relationship, however, has been tested severely throughout campus history. In *Finding God at Harvard*, a compilation of essays from deep-thinking believers in the Harvard community, the story is told of a law school professor who recently made the striking observation that many professors are like "priests who have lost their faith, and kept their jobs." That is what happens when foundations are forgotten. Professors stop professing. Students begin to revolt. The building becomes quite shaky. And the whole story starts to lose its plot.

While later history demonstrates that most colleges and universities drifted from their sacred center and in many ways abandoned the foundations of faith on which they were originally established, history also reveals a riveting story of student movements that have boldly and consistently reminded campuses of their original design. Part two of *God on Campus* tells a number of those stories. In the words inscribed on the original seal of the College of New Jersey, which in time became Princeton University: *Vitam Mortuis Reddo*, "I restore life to the dead."

Part Two

STUDENT MOVEMENTS

Since Jesus' time numberless bands of Christian youth have "turned the world upside down" and thus led [humanity] forward in its struggle for freedom and deeper religious experience. The universities have always been breeding places for such groups.

—CLARENCE P. SHEDD

4

Williams College, 1806. *Usually a few more students gathered to pray under the tall and shady maple trees in Sloan's meadow, but that day there were only five. The summer heat was oppressive, clinging to the late August air like a wet blanket. Dark clouds were gathering in the distance and you could almost taste the coming rain.*

Samuel Mills, the leader of the small collective, seemed hardly to notice the inclement shift in weather. He was far too focused on the conversation at hand to give much concern to the darkening sky. For a number of weeks now, the group had been discussing and debating the pioneering and controversial work of William Carey in South Asia, and considering together whether or not their lives might follow a similar path.

When a bolt of lightning cracked the summer sky and drops of rain began finding their way through the leafy umbrella of the maple trees, the group decided it was time to take their conversation elsewhere. Their initial thought was to make a mad dash all the way back to campus. Midway through their retreat, though, the rain shower started to ease, so they hunkered down by a wet heap of hay in an open field and determined to wait the weather out instead.

The five students—James Richards, Francis Robbins, Harvey Loomis, Byron Green and Samuel Mills—picked up their conversation under the haystack precisely where they had left off in the maple grove. Very specifically, China was the place they had in mind that day, a land so distant and seemingly different from America in the minds of these early nineteenth-century dreamers that it was difficult for them to even imagine what such a faraway country might be like.

Remnants of the electrical storm, with the ominous echo of thunder still beating through the open field that surrounded them, seemed to lend some of its energy to the weighty issues they were pondering.

Mills—just a freshmen himself, but having thought about these things much longer than his friends—made the simple point that their entire conversation and their passionate prayers might all be in vain unless they were willing to give their own lives for the places and people they dreamed about.

The risks they considered were undeniably real. There were no churches or mission agencies in America who would send them, no short-term trips available, and there was very little chance they would ever come home alive. After debating the pros and cons for some time, the group became pensively quiet, thinking about what might actually happen if they seriously attempted to go.

Sam Mills finally butted into the silence: "We can do this," he said, "if we will."

During the next two years the group continued to meet and pray, inviting other like-minded students to join them, finally forming themselves into an official society in September of 1808. Because they met so early in the morning, they initially called themselves Sol Oriens, which is Latin for "The Rising Sun." When they discovered, however, that Sol Oriens was a popular name for Masonic Lodges, they dropped the title and adopted the name Society of the Brethren instead.

The Brethren was a mysterious group at Williams College, keeping records of their meetings in code and, according to their early constitution, requiring all members to "solemnly promise to keep inviolably secret the existence of this society." Their bizarre secrecy stemmed from a deep concern that other students and even local church leaders would look on their convictions as nothing more than fleeting religious fanaticism.

Evidenced in the serious tone of their documents, though, the group's unyielding devotion was clearly more than a passing phase. "Each member shall keep absolutely free from every engagement," records the Brethren's constitution, "which . . . shall be deemed incompatible with the object of this society; and shall hold himself in readiness to go on a mission when and where duty may call."

The sacrificial commitment of the Society of the Brethren was con-

tagious, and similar mission societies began forming at other campuses as well, most notably at Andover Seminary, where Samuel Mills transferred after his graduation from Williams.

At Andover the society took a dramatic step forward when an official petition for overseas missionary service—signed by Adoniram Judson of Brown, Samuel Nott of Union, Samuel Newell of Harvard and Samuel Mills of Williams—was presented to the General Association of the Congregational Churches of Massachusetts on June 27, 1810. From that moment on, the college mission societies were no longer a secret.

Two years later, in the early winter of 1812, the first foreign missionaries from America were ordained for overseas service. Samuel Mills, surprisingly, was not one of them. The newly formed American Foreign Missionary Sending Society specifically requested that Mills stay behind to help stir up student interest in missionary service.

Those who did go—Gordon Hall, Luther Rice, Samuel and Roxana Nott, Samuel and Harriet Newell, and Adoniram and Ann Judson— sailed for Calcutta in February of 1812. Their stories, spread through mission societies now networked across multiple campuses, had an astonishing effect on students, inspiring many of them to commit their lives to the same cause. It was the beginning of the modern American missions movement.

Samuel Mills never forgot his simple commitment to God at the haystack. He continued as an essential leader of this intercollegiate missions movement until he sailed for London on November 16, 1817. While in London, he met with William Wilberforce to discuss what might be done on behalf of African slaves in America. By this point in Mills's life, his extended travels throughout America had convinced him that central to his missionary calling was working toward a practical solution for slavery.

He left London for an exploratory trip to the west coast of Africa in February of 1818, hoping to help create a place where freed slaves might be able to rebuild their lives and govern a free society. The result of this initiative was the nation of Liberia. In a letter to his sister on February 26, 1818, the last letter Mills would ever write, he explained his missionary calling and how it related to slavery in the most practical of terms: "If an evil exists in a community, a remedy must be sought."

While traveling by boat back to England, Samuel Mills died of a respiratory fever on June 16, 1818. His body was buried at sea.*

---

*For more on the Haystack Prayer Meeting and its vital effect on global missions and student involvement, see Gardiner Spring, *Memoirs of Samuel J. Mills*; John H. Hewitt, *Williams College and Foreign Missions*; and Clarence P. Shedd, "Youth Possessed by Dreams," in *Two Centuries of Student Christian Movements*.

PRAYING UNDER A HAYSTACK

EVERYDAY MOMENTS AND
GLOBAL MOVEMENTS

A dark cloud was rising in the west and it soon
began to thunder. . . . [W]e left the grove and went
under the haystack.

—BYRON GREEN

There is no little irony in the fact that both the fiftieth- and one-hundredth-year commemorations of the Haystack Prayer Meeting were rained out by thunderstorms. At the 1856 celebration, which included a big heap of hay and a rebuilt bungalow to help remember the significant moment, a violent downpour completely drenched the festivities. When the centenary anniversary rolled around in 1906, Leverett Spring, historian of Williams College, regrettably records that a heavy storm "broke up the sunrise service." Thankfully, the skies cleared and the sun reappeared before the main ceremony took place later that afternoon, at which 2,500 people were in attendance.

It is strangely fitting, when you really think about it, for celebrations intended to recall an almost rained out student prayer gathering to be met by unwelcome thunderstorms some fifty and one hundred years later. Perhaps it is God's way of helping us remember the vital connection between everyday, inconvenient, ordinary moments and history-making, world-effecting global movements. The Haystack Prayer Meeting, which launched the American foreign missions movement, was just one consecrated moment that involved the ordinary lives of a few devoted college students on a rainy day in Massachusetts. But it represented something much more than that. Those students had a rain-or-shine commitment to God marked by a willingness to go anywhere, at whatever cost, to see Jesus' kingdom come "on earth, as it is in heaven" (Matthew 6:10).

Considering the remarkable history that resulted from the haystack prayer group, we might think that Samuel Mills, the group's leader, was a powerhouse personality who easily attracted others. On the contrary, Mills's roommate at Andover, Timothy Woodbridge, describes him in an 1810 letter as an "awkward figure . . . [with a] croaking sort of voice." Woodbridge continues, "but [Mills] has a great heart and great designs. His great thoughts in advance of his age are not like the dreams of a man who is in a fool's paradise, but they are judicious and wise." Sam Mills's uncanny capacity to inspire others and to believe in possibilities beyond his own abilities did not stem from any evident gift he had on the outside but from a passionate resolve he had on the inside.

LIVING PURPOSEFULLY VERSUS LIVING STUPIDLY

O that I might be aroused from this careless and stupid state, and be enabled to fill up life well!

—SAMUEL MILLS

Judging from Mills's journal entries, it seemed to him that there was a clear choice to be made during one's college career: between living purposefully on the one hand and living stupidly on the other. The following is from the June 25, 1806, entry in his diary, about six weeks before the historic haystack episode:

I shall have an opportunity to [pray] today. . . . O that God would be with me. . . . It will be a stupid time indeed, if the Lord does not pour down his spirit and convince me of my unworthiness.

Four days later, his prayers (which mention the word *stupid* repeatedly) are apparently answered, as Mills records in his journal that he has "never been carried so above the world before. . . . Come, Holy Spirit . . . give me, unworthy me, a spirit of prayer!"

In the purposeful mind of Mills, *stupidity* had less to do with one's test scores (encouraging, isn't it?) and more to do with one's overall life direction. The question was not, Are you making the highest mark in class? but rather, Are you living your life on purpose? Now that did not mean some sort of intentional disengagement from academics, as one of the students most powerfully affected by this purposeful and focused living was Gordon Hall, a Williams College valedictorian in 1809. It did mean, however, that college was not simply a season to merely let life happen to you.

One of the champions of this way of living was Algernon Bailey, a student who preceded Mills at Williams. Utterly dissatisfied with the status quo at college, Bailey became the leader of a small collective of students praying for transformation on campus. He was so passionate in his prayers, in fact, that he eventually became known as "Bailey, mighty in prayer" and was threatened at one point by a group of disgruntled students who said they would mob him if he did not stop praying for them. The effect of such bold prayers was a widespread spiritual awakening at Williams in early 1806. Resulting from that revival were mission minded moments like the Haystack Prayer Meeting and purposeful groups like the Society of the Brethren.

The Brethren was just one of multiple groups that emerged on campuses at the turn of the nineteenth century. There was the Theological Society of Dartmouth and the Yale Moral Society, the College Praying Society of Brown and the club with the hippest name of them all, The Saturday Evening Religious Society in Harvard College. These were part of a surge in student initiatives that endeavored to deal with the theological, social, devotional and missional issues of their day. What made these voluntary societies particularly dynamic was that they began to work together.

CONNECTING THE DOTS

*Perhaps no one finding of this study is quite so important
as the evidence it brings of a basic urge in these societies
for fellowship that is intercollegiate, interdenominational,
and international.*

—CLARENCE P. SHEDD

There is a deep desire in the human heart, common to most people
and especially active in students, to be part of a something bigger,
greater and significantly more lasting than the daily grind of classroom duties and the cyclical patterns of nine-to-five routines. Of
course, there is nothing innately wrong with such duties and routines
(they are, in fact, essential)—but such activities can quickly become
monotonous if they are not infused with a deeper sense of purpose.
Critical to discovering that purpose, as evidenced in the intercollegiate student movement of the early 1800s, is realizing we are not
alone: *There are others who are praying even as we are praying and
they too are believing for and working toward significant change, just
like us.*

Andover and Brown, and later Amherst, were vital student hubs for
connecting the dots of relationship between college societies in the
early nineteenth century. Very early on, groups at these institutions
recognized the vast potential for networking campuses. Most significant in this evolving patchwork of student partnership was the primary focus given to *mission.* Campus historian Clarence Shedd claims
that the "foreign missionary society" was the most influential of all
the societies formed, extending its life much further than the theologi-
cal- or devotional-specific groups. Evidence for this lies in the large
number of campus collectives during this era that adopted the title
Society of Missionary Inquiry (another shockingly cool name).

The global effect of these emerging student-mission initiatives was
especially felt through pioneering educational projects that established primary and secondary schools in the Polynesian islands, parts

of Africa, Latin America and in India. From this same surge of student activism emerged the annual College Day of Prayer (1815), which became a vital force for spiritual awakening in reminding colleges of their original design as institutions with a Christian heritage.

United by common purpose and campus praying, students like Samuel Mills, "Bailey, mighty in prayer," Gordon Hall and Adoniram Judson discovered the exponential strength that comes through working together and the power of unity to affect social change.[*] "These students were doing much more than seeking for hints from other colleges as to how to run their student organizations," explains Shedd in an insightful consideration of the long-term effect of the student mission societies, "they were reaching out across denominational, national, and racial barriers for that sense of solidarity and common cause which in times of greatest vitality has been the most motivating force in the spread of the Christian community."

THE VIRAL EFFECT OF FRIENDSHIP AND PRAYER

Epidemics tip because of the extraordinary efforts of a few select carriers.

—MALCOLM GLADWELL

The history of the Haystack Prayer Meeting is a fascinating case study in helping us understand the viral effect of genuine friendships and global faith. Samuel Mills and his mates surely had no idea how profoundly long-lasting their faith-filled obedience would ultimately be, particularly in the unique way their story continues to influence others to follow their example. Just think of it: here we are, some two hundred years later, still talking about the spiritual legacy of five college students who decided to engage with God on a hot, stormy day in the

---

*There are no women in this list because college education was mostly limited to men during this time. Two critical turning points in the higher education of women came later in the 1800s when Mount Holyoke was officially chartered as a women's seminary in 1836 and when four female students were admitted to Oberlin College in 1837, making it a coed institution.

summer of 1806. That is extraordinary.

Equally extraordinary are the serious social concerns these early nineteenth-century students sought to address, challenge and change during their own lifetime. Notably, one of the most common topics of prayer and debate in their societies was the issue of slavery. Samuel Mills, as noted in the introductory narrative of this chapter, became so concerned about the human injustice of slavery that it led him all the way to the west coast of Africa to try to do something about it.

Now obviously there were plenty of mistakes made along the way, as any honest assessment of mission history should plainly reveal. At the same time, though, these pioneering missionaries became essential characters in the unfolding stories of education and healthcare, language translation and international diplomacy in multiple nations around the world. Adoniram Judson, for example, before he died in Burma in 1850, translated the Bible into Burmese and completed a Burmese dictionary as well. Language translation is an essential force in preserving culture. We will consider this principle more thoroughly in chapter six, when we see how the heritage of the haystack continued to unfold through an historic initiative called the Student Volunteer Movement.

For now, though, it is enough to ponder the viral effect of a few friends and their faith-filled prayers. The Haystack Prayer Meeting was an everyday moment that helped inspire a global movement. "Though you and I are very little beings," Sam Mills once said, "we must not rest . . . till we have made our influence extend to the remotest corner of this . . . world."

FINDING YOUR PLACE IN HISTORY

With [Samuel Mills] the field was the world, and all
nations were made of one blood.

—JOHN H. HEWITT

Taking into account the era of history in which the haystack movement emerged (a period of horses and snail mail, not airplanes and

Facebook), the global reach of Sam Mills and his mates is even more amazing. In some ways, the flood of globalization we have experienced in our own time has numbed us to the wonder of a planet that is more closely connected than ever before. Whether we realize it or not, however, our daily choices *do* impact the rest of the world: through the coffee we purchase, the clothes we wear, the resources we consume and, yes, the prayers we pray. So, what are some key lessons we can take away from an everyday moment under a haystack that resulted in a global movement?

1. Our everyday decisions have the power to influence the world in both big and small ways. Consider the implications of that as it relates to practical areas of justice and injustice in our globalized economy, and also as it relates to how the power of prayer can reach right across the planet.

2. Connect your student collective to a student group that is active on another campus. Talk with each other, get together occasionally, pray for one another and pay attention to the vast potential of what can happen when a few people in a few places commit their everyday, ordinary lives to loving God and loving people.

5

New York City, 1857. *It was three-and-a-half years before the start of the Civil War and even though times were tough in the early autumn of 1857, no one could have imagined the extent of the bloody carnage that was ahead.*

Churches in the middle of the nineteenth century were busy with just trying to keep their members. Disillusionment with religion, some of it resulting from an unfulfilled prophecy that Jesus was returning in 1843, had dealt the attendance rosters of certain congregations a fairly devastating blow.

Politically, people were divided. The most contentious topic of the day was slavery. An agricultural-driven economy in the Southern states had convinced much of the population there that slaves were a necessity for both the livelihood of their plantations and for the balance of power that would be lost if the more industrialized Northern states were entrusted with the national authority to determine laws that were binding on all.

Money, as usual, was the most prominent concern for the majority of the population on both sides of the Mason-Dixon Line. Even in the North, where the abolition movement had deep roots and was becoming increasingly strong, the bank panic of 1857 produced more anxiety in the minds of most Northerners than did any social or human-rights concerns about the powerful institution of Southern slavery.

A financial crisis, spurred on by the Californian gold rush of 1848 and a wave of risky investments that followed, had been building for some time. When the New York branch of the Ohio Life Insurance and Trust Company failed at the end of August in 1857, public confidence in the national financial system was seriously shaken.

By mid-October, the entire banking system collapsed. "No one having large payments to make, without the cash actually in hand," reported the New York Observer on October 15, 1857, "could hope to escape, and but few are in a position not to be severely tried . . ."

> *The poor labourer . . . and the millionaire . . . have found alike the vanity of all earthly independence; thousands daily thrown out of work without a moment's notice; fortunes which have been founded . . . and nurtured through every previous change . . . crumbled or vanished like a dream.*

The Northern states, with their wealth especially dependent on industry, were hit the hardest by the financial crisis. Banks in New York City closed down for a full two months and more than thirty thousand people in the city lost their jobs. In early November a riot broke out on Wall Street and the military was called in to disperse the mob when an angry crowd of unemployed men threatened to force their way into the Treasury Building and take the $20,000,000 in cash reserves that were stored in the vaults.

Before the banking madness broke out on Wall Street, however, an unusual prayer meeting started taking place on Fulton Street, in the financial district of Manhattan.

In the summer of 1857 a businessman named Jeremiah Lanphier was appointed by the North Dutch Reformed Church as an urban missionary to the city of New York. Lanphier's task was straightforward. He was assigned the responsibility of visiting families in the surrounding neighborhoods in hopes of increasing church attendance.

As Lanphier made his rounds in the city, he increasingly took note of the public anxiety that was mounting in the financial district. With a solid background in business, it was natural for Lanphier to understand the stress and concerns associated with economic venture. What was particularly concerning to him, though, was the genuine fear he observed in the eyes of the businessmen he passed on the streets. These men were not just stressed about their jobs; some of them were on the verge of breakdown.

With the permission of his church, Jeremiah Lanphier issued a simple invitation for the businessmen of the city to join him in prayer during their lunchtime break. "How Often Shall I Pray?" read the opening line of the leaflet he distributed:

As often as the language of prayer is in my heart; as often as I see
my need of help; as often as I feel the power of temptation; as
often as I am made sensible of any spiritual declension, or feel
the aggression of a worldly earthly spirit. . . . In prayer, we leave
the business of time for that of eternity, and [conversation] with
men for [conversation] with God.

The other side of the handout plainly outlined the practical details of
the Fulton Street Prayer Meeting:

A day Prayer-Meeting is held every Wednesday from 12 to 1
o'clock in the Consistory building in the rear of the North Dutch
Reformed Church, corner of Fulton and William Streets.

The meeting is intended to give merchants, mechanics, clerks,
strangers and businessmen generally an opportunity to stop and
call upon God amid the perplexities incident to their respective
[occupations]. It will continue for one hour; but it is also designed
for those who may find it inconvenient to remain more than five
or ten minutes, as well as for those who can spare the whole
hour. The necessary interruption will be slight, because antici-
pated, and those who are in haste can often expedite their busi-
ness engagements by halting to lift up their voices to the throne
of grace in humble, grateful prayer.

On September 23, 1857, precisely at noon, Jeremiah Lanphier
opened the doors of the Consistory building. A half-hour passed be-
fore even one person showed up, and by the time the allotted hour
was over there were only six of them in all. The following Wednesday,
however, the six had multiplied to twenty. And by the next week, the
twenty praying people had doubled to forty.

The crowd seemed so encouraged by the prayer that the church
decided to create sacred space every day, rather than just once a
week. By the fourteenth of October, the day the banking system
crashed, over one hundred people were at the Fulton Street Prayer
Meeting.

"Prayer never was such a blessing to me as at this time," explained
one businessman who attended the gatherings, "If I could not get

some half hours every day to pray myself into a right state of mind, then I would certainly either be overburdened or disheartened, and do such things as no Christian . . . ought."

Six months later, even though the financial crisis had been averted, ten thousand people—mainly businessmen—were gathering for prayer everyday in multiple locations throughout New York City. The movement multiplied to other cities across the country, and during the next two years a million people decided to follow Jesus as a result.

The 1857–1858 awakening spread like a holy contagion in collegiate communities, affecting almost every college campus in the nation at that time. The annual College Day of Prayer was especially significant as a starting point for many of the campus prayer movements that began to emerge mid-nineteenth century.

"From its small beginnings," explained the president of Amherst, Dr. Augustus Stearns, in 1858, "[the awakening] made gradual progress until the entire collegiate community was brought under its influence . . . the reformation of character and manners no less remarkable than the renewal of hearts."

Northeastern colleges like Amherst and Yale were joined in their experience of spiritual awakening with Midwestern campuses like the University of Michigan and Wilberforce University, and Southern colleges like Oglethorpe and Wake Forest, Emory and Furman. Most significant during this time as well was the emergence of the Student Young Men's Christian Association at the University of Virginia on October 12, 1858. The College YMCA eventually became a strategic hub for student-led initiatives, particularly in the area of Christian witness and practical service.

Widespread effects of the 1857–1858 awakening, ranging from ethical reforms in business practice to voluntary student involvement in social concerns to heightened engagement in the abolitionary cause, were actively at work when the first shots of the Civil War were fired on Fort Sumter in Charleston, South Carolina, on April 12, 1861. From that moment on, the vital focus of the nation was critically directed toward war.

Even though the prayer movement continued to have profound influence on both sides of the conflict during the next four years, more than 600,000 people would nevertheless die as a result of the War Between the States, many of them students.[*]

---

*The most thorough account of the 1857–1858 awakening is J. Edwin Orr, *The Event of the Century*. Two smaller works that offer a brief overview are J. Edwin Orr, *America's Great Revival* and Bob Eklund, *Spiritual Awakening*. For a nineteenth century glimpse of the movement, see Talbot Chambers, *The New York City Noon Prayer Meeting* (originally published in 1858).

SACRED SPACE AND CIVIL WAR

CAMPUS TRANSFORMATION
AND SOCIAL CHANGE

Human slavery is now doomed in the United States,
doomed to give way, lose confidence, crumble in fatal
demoralization, and finally cease and be a fact forgotten.

—HORACE BUSHNELL, ADDRESSING
A CONGREGATION IN 1857

The fundamental weakness of war is the inability of violence to heal social wounds and bridge cultural divides. For even though slaves were set free after the Civil War, the profound challenge of being black in America was far from over. Justice does not always come quickly and is rarely (if ever) achieved through war. More than a century later, the Civil Rights Movement of the 1960s, the Rodney King riots of 1992 in Los Angeles and the historic election of Barack Obama as the first African American President of the United States in 2008 were all part of our parents' and our own generation's journey in coming to terms with the complicated history of color and culture in America.

In the mid-1800s, 95 percent of African Americans lived in the South, and contrary to some of our hopeful ideas about the North, there were very few white people on either side of the Mason-Dixie Line during those days who viewed our black brothers and sisters as equal members of the human family. It is a perplexing and painful history, wrought with contradictions on every side. Some thought it was best to free the slaves and send them back to Africa, as President Abraham Lincoln proposed. Others, like the editor of the fiery *Liberator* newspaper, William L. Garrison, and the abolitionary theologian Timothy D. Weld, who authored *The Bible Against Slavery* in 1837, worked toward full emancipation and civil rights in America. There were still others who doggedly viewed slavery as the will of God.

Concerns over slavery resulted in particularly heated conversations on college campuses. After a public debate about slavery at Lane Theological Seminary in 1834, during which the differing viewpoints of immediate abolition and recolonization were passionately argued for and against, four-fifths of the student body left the seminary and transferred to Oberlin College. In 1835 Oberlin admitted four African Americans into its student body after its trustees voted "that the education of people of color is a matter of great interest, and should be encouraged and sustained in this institution." The same year at Amherst, the student-led Anti-Slavery Society (of whom all but six were devout followers of Jesus) were instructed by the college overseers to disband because of the controversy they were creating on campus. The students refused, explaining they could not "conscientiously disband and relinquish the right of inquiring into, discussing, and praying over the suffering and woes of more than two million of our population."

The most frustrating aspect of the history surrounding slavery is that Christians, Northern and Southern alike, were on various sides of the issue. The most humbling, and indeed scandalous, aspect of this history is that God apparently visited everyone—slave and free, white and black, North and South—with spiritual awakening before the Civil War broke out and even while it was taking place. The only way I can possibly understand how the 1857–1858 prayer movement transcended the multilayered social and cultural differences that so deeply divided our nation is in the simple knowledge that *God is not prejudiced*. Indeed, could it be that God mercifully visited the entire population—the powerful and the poor—in hopes that prayer might save us from war?

WHEN THE POWERFUL AND THE POOR PRAY AS ONE

Slavery is primarily the church's sin, because the very fact
that pastors and professing Christians from different
denominations hold slaves is what sanctifies the whole
abomination. . . . If the church united against slavery,
within three years there would be not be a shackled slave
or a cruel slaveholder in our country.

—CHARLES FINNEY

It is very significant that even as the businessman's prayer movement was emerging on Fulton Street in New York City, there was an active spiritual awakening taking place on Anson Street in Charleston, South Carolina. Most fascinating about the Charleston awakening is that it started as a prayer meeting in a Presbyterian congregation that was mostly attended by black communicants. The white minister Dr. John L. Girardeau decided not to preach at the prayer meetings but to instead wait "for the outpouring of the Spirit," in the words of an 1899 biography about Girardeau's life.

While waiting one evening in prayer, something akin to an electrical surge struck Dr. Girardeau in the head and sent a charge through his entire frame. "For a little while," his biography records, "he stood speechless under the strange physical feeling." Then he said:

"The Holy Spirit has come. We will begin preaching tomorrow evening." He closed the service with a hymn and dismissed the congregation, and came down from the pulpit; but no one left the house. . . . [H]e [soon] realized the situation. The Holy Spirit had not only come to him, [but] had also taken possession of the hearts of the people. . . . [H]e began exhorting them to accept the Gospel. They began to sob softly, like the falling of rain; then with deeper emotion to weep bitterly or to rejoice loudly, according to circumstance. It was midnight before he could dismiss the congregation.

During the next eight weeks, crowds comprising both blacks and whites, as large as fifteen hundred to two thousand people, attended the services. Simultaneously, the Fulton Street Prayer Meeting was spreading rapidly throughout New York City and beginning to have effect in multiple urban settings across the nation. At a prayer gathering in Boston, for example, an out-of-town attendee offered a striking testimony of how widespread the movement had become. "I am from Omaha, Nebraska," the visitor explained, "On my journey east I have found a continuous prayer meeting all the way . . . a prayer meeting about two thousand miles in extent."

Consider the phenomenon—poor slaves in Charleston, South Carolina, and powerful businessmen in New York City joined together through a continuous movement of prayer that stretched from Omaha to Boston, from New York to Charleston. Now add to that stunning social dynamic of prayer the raw energy of young people, representing almost every college in the country at that time and soon to be in critical positions of influence in society, and we can begin to appreciate the very real potential of how campus transformation can result in social change.

CAMPUS PRAYER CONTAGION

The Yale revival started on the day of prayer for colleges
and, according to the testimony of Mr. H. E. Barnes and
Mr. E. B. Furbish, both of the class of 1860, was
characterized by multiplied and crowded prayer-
meetings, which sometimes embraced every member of
a given college class. There were no special preachers.

—TWO CENTURIES OF CHRISTIAN ACTIVITY AT YALE

Particularly noteworthy in the 1857–1858 awakening was the absence of any one leader or famous preacher at the center of the movement. Evangelist Charles Finney was especially well known *before* the awakening, and the ministry of D. L. Moody was in some ways launched *out* of the awakening, but there was no central leader actively directing the prayer movement *during* the awakening. This decentralized characteristic was especially at work on college campuses, enabling students (not visiting evangelists) to become the contagious carriers of the prayer virus.

To understand just how widespread the student prayer movement was during this time, it is helpful to list some of the campuses that were involved:

Oberlin	University of Virginia	Mary Sharp
Dartmouth	Ingham	Mount Lebanon
Middlebury	Davidson	Baylor
Amherst	University of North	University of
Brown	Carolina	Michigan
Yale	University of South	Ohio Wesleyan
Columbia	Carolina	Denison
Union	College of	Kenyon
Genesee	Charleston	Wilberforce
Madison	Furman	Wabash College
Hamilton	Wofford	DePauw
Elmira	Emory	Indiana University
Rutgers	University of	Illinois College
Princeton	Georgia	Shurtleff
Penn	Oglethorpe	Beloit
Jefferson	Mercer	William Jewell

At the start of the Civil War there were about 250 colleges in America, having increased from just nine chartered colleges at the start of the Revolutionary War. Even though a number of these pioneering initiatives in education did not long survive, the 1857–1858 awakening nevertheless affected the majority of them.

As was the case during the Great Awakening of the 1700s, new colleges were founded during this time of spiritual transformation. Passionate Presbyterians founded the College of California in 1855, which in time merged with the Agricultural, Mining and Mechanical Arts College to form the University of California at Berkeley. (Written into the very DNA of Berkeley's original design, in fact, was "the discourse of reason, intelligence, and *faith*.") Christians inspired by the 1857–1858 prayer movement also started Chapman College in Los Angeles in 1861. Reaching well beyond campus prayer meetings and business-men awakenings, the movement soon extended its influence into critical areas of social and global change as well.

CREATING CONSCIENCE THROUGH PRAYER: SOCIAL AND GLOBAL EFFECTS

The revival moved out to sea, and ships became floating mission stations to ports around the world. Ships, as they drew near American ports, came within a definite zone of spiritual intensity. Ship after ship arrived with the same story of conviction and conversion.

—BOB L. EKLUND

As news of the awakening spread, a similar sort of movement emerged in the north of Ireland and Scotland in 1859, as well as in England by 1860. "One of the first effects of the awakening [in the U.K.]," writes J. Edwin Orr, "was the creation of a new and intense sympathy with the poor and suffering." The most well-known and long-lasting initiative that emerged in England during this time was the evangelistic and social work of William and Catherine Booth, even-tually known as The Salvation Army.

Witnessing the incredible results of the awakening in England, a struggling thirty-three-year-old British missionary named Hudson Taylor (who was at home in London while on leave from China) deter-mined to start the China Inland Mission. The CIM soon became the model for a surge of interdenominational mission movements founded throughout the nineteenth and twentieth centuries.

Considering the remarkable social influence of the awakening over-seas, we cannot help but wonder why the 1857–1858 prayer movement was not able to prevent the war in America. One possible answer is that influential figures both North and South interpreted the presence of God as favor for their political position, rather than mercy despite their sin. "The Civil War, as a consequence," writes Mark Noll in *Old Religion in the New World*, "[became] a religious war." Claiming God is on your side in war is a dangerous position to take regardless of where you stand.

FINDING YOUR PLACE IN HISTORY

Why did not the 1857–1858 Awakening make impossible the fratricidal slaughter of the Civil War?

—J. EDWIN ORR

J. Edwin Orr's question is one of the most important points we must consider when thinking about the potential of campus transformation and social change. Although I may be wrong, I cannot help but hope that given enough time and prayer, diligent thinking and honest conversations, courageous work and sacrificial commitment, even the greatest of evils can finally be overcome by love. (William Wilberforce did it in his day, why should we not be able to do it in ours?) The Civil War preserved the Union, but it failed to transform hearts and minds, on *either* side of the conflict. That is why more than 140 years down the road, we still have a long road to walk in the journey of understanding color and culture in America, and around the world.

1. Think about what you perceive to be the most important social issue of our day. What are you doing about it?

2. If you are doing something about it, have you taken the time to learn from someone who sees the issue differently than you do? Demonizing the other side creates very little sacred space for the power of relationship to affect change.

3. Finally, gather some friends and listen to God for creative ways to engage with the issue. You may be surprised by how simply and practically God leads you.

6

Northfield, Massachusetts, 1886.

The turnout surprised everyone: 251 college students from 86 campuses representing 26 states. Even though the invitation was only sent three months before, students gathered from all over the country to spend the month of July at the Mount Hermon Bible Conference in Northfield, Massachusetts.

"I have been asked for programs," the booming voice of D. L. Moody announced at the opening meeting. Smiling beneath his burly grey beard and eyeballing the students one-by-one, the big-bellied fifty-year-old evangelist laughed and continued:

> *I hate programs and I don't have any. Then I can't break over them. If you want to know what is ahead, we don't know except that we will have a good time. We want to stir you up and get you in love with the Bible, and those of you who have a voice, in love with music.*
>
> *If I find you getting drowsy in this hot weather, I will just ask the speaker to stop and we will sing. Now about questions—our talks are going to be conversational. If you want to ask a question, speak out; that's what we're here for, to get all the cobwebs swept away and go back to our college mates inspired with the truth.*

Moody was famous for his down-to-earth understanding of what it means to follow Jesus. He never could bear the idea of a boring God. During one of his meetings in London, in fact, when an overly eager clergyman prayed on and on and on, Moody finally stepped to the stage and invited everyone to join in a hymn while "our brother is finishing his prayer."

It was that sort of refreshing frankness that helped draw so many college students together in the summer of 1886. They came because they expected D. L. Moody and the other leaders to honestly and openly deal with the questions put to them. They came because they believed the Mount Hermon meetings would be different. They came because a month in New England with likeminded friends and a schedule open to God seemed like a pretty good way to spend a summer.

On July 6, 1886, 251 college students showed up at the Mount Hermon Bible Conference with high expectations and malleable hearts.

The summer gathering was not Moody's idea. It was actually the brainchild of a young man named Luther Wishard, a graduate of Princeton commissioned by the newly formed YMCA to network and expand the college fellowships active on campuses across the country. In 1877, with an annual salary of $250 for him and his wife to live on, Wishard began traveling to colleges throughout America to help shape the emerging collegiate network.

During a trip to Williams College in 1883 Wishard experienced a defining moment at the site that marked the spot of the 1806 Haystack Prayer Meeting. Writing of what took place in his heart that day as he stood in front of the marble monument, Wishard recorded that he "made an unreserved surrender" to God—specifically praying, "I am willing to go anywhere, at any time, to do anything for Jesus."

Inspired by the story of Samuel Mills and the other haystack students, Wishard and his wife were eager to give their lives in missionary service overseas, but it was the conviction they could accomplish more for missions by effectively networking an intercollegiate student movement in the States that kept them stationed in America.

By March 1886, a month before Wishard and his coworker Charles Ober approached D. L. Moody about hosting a summer conference, the YMCA student work had gathered such momentum that Wishard wrote in a college periodical: "This Christian Movement among students is too mighty in its power for good to be limited to any country or continent. It will not have fulfilled its mission," he concluded, "until every living student shall, through its agency, have been invited to Christ."

Now even though Wishard was truly convinced something special was emerging on college campuses, Moody was initially skeptical of the idea of a summer gathering. He was especially concerned that young people would not want to give up their summer holidays for a Bible conference in Massachusetts.

Wishard's earnest conviction about the potential of the conference was infectious, however, and he eventually convinced the aging evangelist that it was worth the risk of attempting to gather as many students as they could.

"Well," Moody finally relented in April 1886, "I guess we'd better try it."

Once Moody was on board for the summer, Wishard and Ober immediately sent an invitation to every campus contact they had, as well as dividing eastern and southern sections of the country between them in an attempt to visit as many colleges as they could. At Cornell, Ober recruited a young man named John Mott for the summer gathering, and Wishard urged a Princeton senior named Robert Wilder to join them in Massachusetts as well.

On July 3, when Wishard finally arrived at Mount Hermon, an enthusiastic Ober met him at the local depot and exclaimed, "such an avalanche of students [have] come that we [will] probably have to overflow the haymows."

The pace of the gathering was casual and relaxed, with voluntary meetings in the morning, athletics in the afternoon and plenty of free time too. Moody's leadership and Bible teaching were central to the program, and a period for evening reflection on a hill overlooking the Connecticut Valley was especially critical for many of the life decisions that were made during the conference. Day after day—through steady teaching, honest conversations and open prayer—students gave themselves to God in increasing depth.

It soon became evident that an emphasis on missionary service was emerging at the gathering. The focus did not come from Moody or anyone else at the front, but was the initiative of a few likeminded students from Princeton and Cornell, Oberlin and Harvard. Most influential among these mission-minded students was Robert Wilder.

Born in India to missionary parents, Wilder and his sister, Grace, had been praying for a student missions movement to influence the campuses of America for some time. At Princeton, Wilder was the leader of the Foreign Missionary Society, a small group of students who had committed themselves to overseas service. Each member of the group had signed a declaration of purpose that read: "We are willing and desirous, God permitting, to become foreign missionaries."

During the Mount Hermon Conference, Wilder's enthusiasm about missions began to multiply to others. Looking back on the gathering years later, John Mott recalled, "Early in the conference [Wilder] began to find out [who was] interested in missions. . . . [F]ourteen [of us] met. Soon there were twenty-one. . . . Gradually [this] group became the spiritual and missionary dynamic of the [entire] conference."

Conversations about global mission became so absorbing, in fact, that Wilder finally approached Moody with the idea of an evening meeting wholly committed to understanding the needs of the world. As a result, ten students of diverse backgrounds led a very significant event at Mount Hermon called "The Meeting of Ten Nations."

In three-minute blocks, the students outlined the spiritual needs of the lands they represented, with each one closing their presentation with the words "God is love," spoken in multiple languages. Of the ten who led the meeting, three of them were raised on the mission field in India, China and Persia; six of them were international students representing Armenia, Japan, Thailand, Norway, Denmark and Germany; and one of them was a Native American.

"Seldom have I seen an audience under the sway of God's Spirit as it was that night," Robert Wilder later recorded. "The [students] withdrew to their rooms or went out under [the] trees to wait on God for guidance. . . . During the eight days that followed," he continued, "there were great searchings of heart and great resolves."

By July 30, the closing day of the gathering, ninety-nine students had signed a mission pledge similar to the Declaration of Purpose from Princeton. The next morning, during an impromptu time of farewell prayer, one more student joined the ranks of the ninety-nine, making them exactly one hundred strong. In time, this group became known as the "Mount Hermon One Hundred." *

---

*For more on this fascinating period of student history, see Ruth Wilder Braisted, *In this Generation: The Story of Robert P. Wilder*; Timothy C. Wallstrom, *The Creation of a Student Movement to Evangelize the World*; Laurie Fortunak, ed., *The Evangelization of the World in This Generation: The Hope and Teachings of Robert P. Wilder*; and Lon Allison, ed., *John R. Mott: That the World May Believe.*

LEARNING TO LIVE FOR THE IMPOSSIBLE

THE MOUNT HERMON ONE HUNDRED

Has any such offering of living young men and women
been presented in our age, in our country, in any age, or
in any country, since the days of Pentecost?

—JOHN McCOSH, PRESIDENT OF PRINCETON
(1868–1888)

At first glance, the assessment of President McCosh seems a bit exaggerated. One hundred students committed to missions may be encouraging, but is not necessarily historic. It must be understood, however, that within a generation of the 1886 summer gathering on D. L. Moody's property in Massachusetts, one hundred thousand students were part of the Student Volunteer Movement (SVM) that emerged from Mount Hermon, and twenty-one thousand of those students were sent from North American colleges into missionary service overseas. Perhaps President McCosh was correct in his assessment after all.

Especially fascinating as it relates to the early history of the SVM is the fact that multiple student movements materialized in various locations around the world at about the same time. During the years of 1883 and 1884, for example, just two years before the Mount Hermon conference took place in Massachusetts, there were similar student movements at work in Norway, Sweden, Denmark and Great Britain. "It seems clear," claimed Robert Wilder in hindsight, "that the source of the modern missionary uprising among students must have been in Heaven, appearing as it did on earth at the same time in lands so remote as Scandinavia, Great Britain and North America."

In England and the United States, the movement was especially influenced by the work of D. L. Moody. It all began when three hundred Cambridge students sought the help of the famous evangelist in reaching their campus. In 1882, when Moody at last agreed to come to the venerable center of British learning, the blue-collared American preacher arrived on campus with grave uncertainties as to whether his meetings would be effective at all. "There never was a place," Moody later said, "that I approached with greater anxiety than Cambridge. Never having had the privilege of a university education, I was nervous about meeting university men."

Although the Cambridge meetings started very poorly, with hundreds of students attending for no other reason but to mock the accent of the informal American minister, there was a decided shift when one of the ringleaders of the rowdy students made his way to Moody's lodging late one night to apologize for how they had treated him. The young man's humility spread and before long a number of respected intellectuals and well-known athletes at the university committed their lives to Jesus. When eighteen hundred people showed up for the final night of the Cambridge meetings, Moody looked into the eyes of the eager young crowd and glimpsed the potential of a movement. "My God," the preacher was heard whispering in prayer that night, "this is enough to live for."

It was during this time that two famous Cambridge athletes, C. T. Studd and Stanley Smith, decided to follow Jesus. These two student athletes became the most influential figures in a small collective of Christians called the Cambridge Seven, a group of college friends who committed their lives to missionary service in China. The story of the Cambridge Seven spread like wildfire throughout the United Kingdom, Canada and the United States, and was in time a defining factor in inspiring the radical Christ-centered commitment of Robert Wilder and the Mount Hermon One Hundred.

THE WILDER COMMITMENT

Three or four days before the close of the [Mount
Hermon] Conference, Charles Ober . . . suggested . . . that
a deputation of students be sent among the colleges of
North America, even as the Cambridge Seven had
recently sent a deputation throughout England.

—TIMOTHY WALLSTROM

On August 2, 1886, three days after the summer gathering at Mount Hermon concluded, *The Springfield Republican*, a local newspaper, reported that five students were chosen to travel to as many campuses as possible to tell the story of the Mount Hermon One Hundred. The delegates selected were Robert Wilder of Princeton, John Mott of Cornell, William Taylor of Yale, L. M. Riley of De Pauw and Kotaro N. Shimo-Mura of the Worcester Polytechnic Institute. Upon hearing about their plans, D. W. Williams, a New York City businessman, decided to finance their entire journey.

Everything was proceeding as planned until shortly before the appointed time for travel. Through an unusual chain of events and because of various personal reasons, every member of the traveling band but Wilder determined they were unable to actually take the trip. By this point, even Wilder was seriously considering abandoning the idea. His father was in exceptionally poor health and had only been given six months to live. After two days of careful prayer and consideration of what it might mean for his son to never see him alive again, Robert's sick father called him into his study and said, "Son, let the dead bury their dead, go and preach the kingdom."*

Witnessing the faith of his father, Robert Wilder determined that even if he must travel alone, God had called him to tell the story of the Mount Hermon One Hundred. Fortunately, before Wilder left on his solo mission, one of his friends from Princeton, John Forman, decided

---

*During his own student days at Andover Seminary, Royal G. Wilder (Robert's father) was a member of the Brethren Society, the missions-minded student group started by Samuel Mills as a result of the Haystack Prayer Meeting.

to make the journey with him. Starting in Maine, Wilder and Forman soon set out on the very first college road trip.

During the next eight months, mainly on horseback, these two students visited 162 campuses. Telling the story of the Mount Hermon One Hundred and sharing essential facts about world mission with every student they met, they trailblazed a college mission awakening across North America. By the end of their journey, Wilder and Forman were utterly exhausted but deeply satisfied. Over two thousand students had added their names to the missions-movement pledge.

The summer of 1887 "brought as an encore performance the second Student Summer School" in Massachusetts and from that point forward, collegiate gatherings were annually held in Northfield. During the summer of 1888, the Student Volunteer Movement was officially launched as an intercollegiate network committed to foreign missions. By 1891, the year of the first International Convention, the SVM represented more than six thousand students. The Wilder commitment had become a movement.

One of the reasons the work of Wilder and Forman was so very effective in that defining first year is because they challenged students to "come" and not simply to "go." They never asked of others what they were not completely committed to themselves. Each of them, in fact, eventually moved to India for long-term mission service. Wilder and Forman imparted to others contagious conviction about the needs of the world because they honestly believed in the possibility of what had become the influential watchword of the student movement: *The evangelization of the world in this generation.*

LIVING BY THE WATCHWORD

I can truly answer that next to the decision to take Christ as the leader and Lord of my life, the watchword has had more influence than all other ideals and objectives combined to widen my horizon and enlarge my conception of the kingdom of God.

—JOHN MOTT

For a generation like ours—searching for spiritual meaning but wary of religious exclusivity—"the evangelization of the world in this generation" might sound somewhat arrogant, perhaps a little naive or maybe just plain impossible. After all, many of us have been steeped in historical theories that mainly equate *missions* with the cause of colonizers and *evangelism* with the exploits of Western imperialists. While it is regrettably true that followers of Jesus have often failed to reflect the humility of their master, and great harm has sometimes followed as a result, it is equally true that an honest and careful study of the history of missions also reveals a compelling depth of compassionate foresight and humble conviction.

Consider, for example, John Mott, the young man from Cornell who went on to become the primary leader of the Student Volunteer Movement and who was eventually awarded the Nobel Peace Prize in 1946. "He was never an American bringing an evangelical message to Poland, to South America, or to the East, in an American style," explained the Nobel representative, Herman Ingebretsen, in presenting the award to Mott. "He was an apostle of a simple Christianity, presented in a form which made it living and real to the people to whom it was addressed."

Embracing a global perspective in the cause of Christ was certainly not an easy journey for John Mott. As the SVM expanded around the world in its early years, Mott soon realized the lack of wisdom in using U.S. military metaphors in describing the worldwide hopes of the movement. During a defining and historic gathering that Mott led in Scotland in 1910—an event called the "World Missionary Conference" that gathered 1,355 delegates—a courageous attendee from India, V. S. Azariah, boldly articulated a critical change that must take place in the global missions movement. "You have given your goods to feed the poor. You have given your bodies to be burned," Azariah told the Western leaders, "We also ask for love. *Give us friends.*"

At this significant gathering in Scotland, through a few prophets like Azariah, it began to slowly dawn on the "Christian" West that they were meant to be *in partnership* with the rest of the world rather than *in charge* of the rest of the world. That important shift in perspective represented a very significant development in the modern history of Christianity. "Christ has not revealed Himself solely or fully through any one nation, race or communion," John Mott would in time conclude, "still less through any one individual or group. No part of mankind has a monopoly on His unsearchable riches."

Mott was coming to terms with the vital understanding that evangelism is finally about Jesus. Everything else, including our nationality, is secondary to the centrality of Christ. When Christians operate in that sort of Christ-centeredness, humbly telling people about Jesus instead of forcefully pushing a cultural agenda, we become a vital force for preserving culture rather than crushing culture.

Lamin Sanneh, a West African professor at Yale University, has demonstrated this point powerfully through his fascinating research on the culture-preserving effect of missionaries who translated the New Testament—that is, the story of Jesus—into indigenous languages all around the world. Had it not been for the work of such missionaries, hundreds of languages would have been lost forever through the unyielding and forward march of globalization—a march, we must understand, that was taking place *with or without* missionary involvement.

Even though the SVM had it faults, the movement was never stronger than when it boldly lived by its watchword, "the evangelization of the world in this generation." During that time, thousands of student volunteers lived and died for what seemed to be an impossible dream because they truly believed—through the life of Jesus— that another world was possible. They pioneered schools in Central Africa and preached the gospel in remote villages in South America; they founded hospitals in South Asia and worked toward reconciliation in the heart of Europe. Even when the tragedy of World War I struck, a time that would severely test their resolve and challenge their optimism, as long as the SVM stay focused on Jesus, nothing seemed impossible.

KEEPING THE MAIN THING THE MAIN THING

Why is it important to see Jesus? Because to see Him is
to see God.

—ROBERT WILDER

The Gospels of Matthew, Mark and Luke each record a significant experience in the life of Jesus that became a defining moment for his closest friends and followers. In New Testament history, the event is referred to as the Transfiguration, where before the eyes of Peter, James and John, the down-to-earth appearance of Jesus was transformed by heavenly light. Because of this experience and many others, the disciples ultimately concluded that in seeing Jesus, they had seen the very face of God (Matthew 17:1-8; Mark 9:2-8; Luke 9:29-36).

That extraordinary account from the New Testament is particularly important to the story of the SVM because the Mount Hermon Bible Conference borrowed its name from the Mount of Transfiguration. It was on Mount Hermon—the one in ancient Israel, not the one in Massachusetts—that the transfiguration of Jesus took place. And even as those first-century disciples experienced something on the original Mount Hermon that forever transformed their understanding of God, so the students at the 1886 Mount Hermon Bible Conference experienced a transforming encounter with Jesus that forever changed them too.

In the early days of the movement, the SVM kept their transforming experience of Jesus strong through three essential activities: they paid careful attention to prayer, they seriously studied the Bible, and they actively sought the empowering of the Holy Spirit. This was the SVM way of intentionally staying focused on Jesus, or in other words, keeping the main thing, the main thing.

"Prayer and missions are as inseparable as faith and works," John Mott said at the International Convention in 1902, "in fact, prayer and missions are faith and works." To their dying days, the founding leaders of the SVM insisted that prayer was the secret of the movement. For figures like Wilder and Mott, prayer was much more than a random religious exercise to appease a distant god or some sort of spiritual rite they must undergo before the practical business of a meeting began. Rather, prayer was the very source of their life in God: the *quiet communion* through which they found the grace to surrender their wills to Jesus in the first place and the *relational lifeline* by which they discovered the wisdom to guide a global movement once it began. "[The] Movement owes everything to prayer," Mott confessed, "It was conceived in days and nights of prayer at Mount Hermon . . . [and] has marked every important step in [its] development."

Taking into account the profound effect of prayer on the SVM during its pioneering period at Mount Hermon, we must also keep in mind that the 1886 catalytic summer conference was originally billed as a Bible conference. D. L. Moody, remember, told those 251 college students gathered in Massachusetts that the reason they were there was to, "get . . . in love with the Bible . . . to get all the cobwebs swept away and go back to our college mates inspired with the truth."

Even though such language might sound shallow to some, the intellectual depth of the SVM's academic integrity and their serious attention to biblical scholarship reveals a decidedly different perspective. A classic example of this was when the conservative-leaning Moody invited his liberal-leaning Scottish friend Professor Henry Drummond to be the main speaker at the 1887 summer gathering in Northfield. At the time, Drummond was especially well known for his book *Natural Law in the Spiritual World*, which sought to reconcile science and theology, creation and evolution.

While intentional prayer and careful Bible study were clearly essential in the life of the student volunteers, historian Clarence Shedd notes an even more dynamic factor that vitally shaped the life of the movement during its earliest days at Mount Hermon. Shedd writes of an "experience of consecration and spiritual renewal [that] fell upon scores of the conference delegates" which resulted in a "spontaneous convergence of prayer and discussion upon the subject of foreign missions." These students did not sacrificially give their lives to global mission simply because it seemed like a good idea, but because they were convinced the Holy Spirit was leading them to do so.

Here again the commitment of Robert Wilder was an example to all the rest. Two years before Mount Hermon, in the beginning of his junior year at Princeton, Wilder experienced a significant turning point in his relationship with God. He was attending a meeting in Connecticut and was deeply moved by the teaching of A. J. Gordon, a minister from Boston. When Wilder approached Gordon about the powerful source of his preaching, the older man looked young Wilder in the eye and smiled as he said: "God is ready to give you the power of the Holy Spirit as soon as you are ready to surrender fully to him." Robert Wilder returned to Princeton a different person. And the rest is history.

FINDING YOUR PLACE IN HISTORY

The world has yet to see what God will do with and for and through and in and by the [person] who is fully and wholly consecrated to him.

—HENRY VARLEY

Particularly interesting in the story of the Student Volunteer Movement is the little known fact that the very first student volunteers—those who signed a pledge that they were "willing and desirous" to serve as foreign missionaries—were not the Mount Hermon One Hundred or even the few students at Princeton who were part of Robert Wilder's Mission Society. The original student volunteers emerged at Mount Holyoke, a seminary for young women, where Robert's sister, Grace, graduated from in 1883. Under her inspiring leadership, years before the summer gathering at Mount Hermon took place, thirty-four young women signed their names to a simple pledge and surrendered their lives to the cause of global mission. In time, tens of thousands followed their example and the SVM soon extended its influence around the world. How appropriate that a movement marked by such Jesus-centered surrender all began with a student named Grace.

1. In the words of Luther Wishard, a willingness to "go anywhere, at

any time, to do anything for Jesus" is what constitutes an "unreserved surrender" to God. Does that sort of commitment describe you?

2. We must always remember that evangelism is essentially about Jesus. The goal is not to convert people to our cultural understanding of Christianity but to introduce people to the life of Christ. May it be said of us, as a student once said of Robert Wilder, "I never heard anyone speak of Jesus Christ as he did."

3. For a real-life glimpse into the sort of commitment the Student Volunteer Movement inspired in students and the global effect it ultimately had on their lives, go to the Vimeo website and view "101-yr-old" (www.vimeo.com/3036051). The video is of Dr. Marshall Welles, who signed the SVM pledge during his college days in the 1920s. You won't be disappointed.

7

Yale, 1905. *Most college freshmen are not millionaires, but William Borden was different. Even though he did his best to act as if he was just like every other incoming student when he arrived on campus, Borden's affluent background and privileged history were hard to hide.*

Shortly before the Civil War, William's grandfather, Gail Borden, invented a simple process to condense milk, which kept milk from spoiling. When the Union Army contracted Gail Borden and his financial partner to supply large quantities of condensed milk during the war, Borden's practical invention became a booming business. Before long, Gail Borden was known as the "milkman to the nation."

By the turn of the century the Borden family company surpassed $10 million in sales. Thus, when seventeen-year-old William was accepted into Yale, tuition costs and living expenses were certainly not a challenge for him.

William's wealthy parents, in fact, had just spent a small fortune on a high school graduation gift for their son, treating him and a traveling tutor to a trip around the world. Young Borden and his teacher, Walter Erdman, experienced the time of their lives on the yearlong journey, soaking in sulfur baths in Japan and touring the Taj Mahal in India, floating down the famous canals of Venice and climbing the Great Pyramids of Cairo.

Also during this twelve-month trip Borden began to seriously ponder the question of his calling. Shortly before he returned home, William wrote a letter to his mother about a book by Robert Speer that was significantly shaping his thoughts. "I especially noticed the two chapters [Speer] takes to the Student Volunteer Movement," Borden wrote, "There is something inspiring in the project to me. . . . When I got through reading, I knelt right down and prayed more earnestly than I have for some time."

In his first few days at Yale, Borden met Charley Campbell, who in time became his closest friend. Although Campbell was initially intimidated by Borden's global experiences and family wealth, he soon realized that "Bill" Borden was much more down-to-earth than he originally thought. *"I think of one evening when we staged a complete track-meet in my room,"* Campbell wrote of his freshmen days at Yale with Borden, *"and Bill was the heavy competitor in all the events possible."*

During their first semester, these two friends began praying with each other, a practice they continued throughout their college years. *"It was well on in the first term when Bill and I began to pray together in the morning before breakfast,"* Campbell wrote:

> I cannot say positively whose suggestion it was, but I feel sure it must have originated with Bill. We had been meeting only a short time when a third, Farrand Williams, joined us and soon after a fourth, James M. Howard. The time was spent in prayer after a brief reading of Scripture. Our object was to pray for . . . [the] class and college, and also for those of our friends we were seeking to bring to Christ.

Alongside their rhythms of prayer and conversations about the Bible, there were also a couple of conferences that especially influenced the lives of Bill Borden and his friends during their freshmen year at Yale. The first of these conferences was the SVM student gathering held in Nashville in 1906.

During their long train ride south for the conference, the small delegation of Yale students passed the time with multiple rounds of a game called "hot-hand." According to Campbell's description of the game, "The man who was 'it' must face the side of the car, with his eyes closed. . . . [A]nyone [then] was at liberty to take a whack. After each impact he had to guess who it was that hit him. If his guess was correct," Campbell continued, "the [hitter] had to change places with him; if incorrect, another whack was in order."

The boisterous group arrived in Nashville a little bruised, but in very good spirits. During their few days at the conference, the SVM teacher *that especially influenced Borden was Dr. Samuel Zwemer. "It is not an expedition of ease nor a picnic excursion to which we are called," Zwemer challenged the students, "It is going to cost many a life, and not lives only, but prayers and tears and blood."*

In the summer holidays between his freshman and sophomore year, Borden participated in another student gathering under the leadership of Dr. Henry Wright. Borden's journal entries describe the profound effect of those summer days, recording the simple but transformative understanding of discipleship that was taking place in his life. "Say 'no' to self and 'yes' to Jesus every time," Borden wrote in his journal:

> *In every [person's] heart there is a throne and a cross. If Christ is on the throne, self is on the cross; and if self, even a little bit, is on the throne, Jesus is on the cross in that [person's] heart. . . . If Jesus is on the throne, you will go where He wants you to go. . . . Lord Jesus, I take my hands off, as far as my life is concerned. I put Thee on the throne in my heart.*

After the summer break, Borden returned for his sophomore year at Yale more focused than ever. One of the upperclassmen, Kenneth Latourette, who in time became a famous historian, especially noted the boldness that marked Borden during these days. "In his sophomore year," Latourette wrote about his younger friend:

> *We organized Bible-study groups and divided up the class of three hundred or more, each [person] interested taking a certain number, so that all might, if possible, be reached. The names were gone over one by one, and the question asked, "Who will take this person or that?" When it came to one who was a hard proposition there would be an ominous pause. Nobody wanted the responsibility. Then Bill's voice would be heard: "Put him down to me."*

The steady faith and boldness of Borden produced remarkable results. What started as a simple exercise of prayer and Bible study for him and Charley Campbell in the early mornings of their freshmen year, ultimately evolved into a campuswide awakening by the time they were seniors. When Borden graduated in 1909, one thousand of Yale's thirteen hundred students were gathering weekly for prayer.

The campus, though, was not the only place where Borden directed his attention during his college career. New Haven, Connecticut, the city where Yale is located, was home to an increasing number of homeless drunks in the early 1900s. To take care of these individuals and begin the process of their rehabilitation, Borden started the Yale Hope Mission during his junior year in 1907.

"I never knew a feller just like Bill," explained one of the men transformed through the mission, "the way he came [to] us, you would never think he was a man of wealth. . . . It couldn't seem possible a man could be so humble and yet so great. He could talk to anyone," the man said, "didn't matter who they was. And he'd get down with his arms round the poor burly bum and hug him. . . . Never knowed his like in the world. I know he must have done for hundreds just what he done for me."

After completing his undergraduate work at Yale, Borden went on to graduate studies at Princeton Seminary. In 1912, when he was ordained for missionary service at Moody Church in Chicago, a number of newspapers carried the story of his ordination. The headlines especially drew attention to the incongruity between Borden's privileged background and his intended field of service in a remote and impoverished region of northwest China.

Even though Borden never read the stories, the public acclaim was particularly embarrassing for him. "I am sorry there was such unnecessary publicity," he wrote in a letter to his Princeton friends, "and hope you fellows will discount what was said."

On December 17, 1912, Borden set sail for Asia. Because he intended to work with Chinese Muslims in the province of Gansu, he journeyed first to Egypt to study Arabic. Unfortunately, during his brief sojourn in Cairo, he contracted spinal meningitis through a bacterial infection.

For two long weeks, under the watchful eye of his missionary hero, Dr. Samuel Zwemer, Borden wrestled for his life. Tragically, on April 9, 1913, William Borden died. He was twenty-five years old. When word of his death reached the United States, almost every newspaper in the nation carried the story.

Shortly after William Borden died, his Bible was given to his mother. Inscribed on the inside cover were three simple statements:

No reserves.

No retreats.

*No regrets.**

---

*Because his family was already cared for, William Borden left his entire fortune to local and global mission work. By current financial standards, that fortune represented more than $50 million. For more on the brief but remarkable life of William Borden, see Mrs. Howard Taylor, *Borden of Yale '09: The Life That Counts*; Dick Bohrer, *Bill Borden: The Finished Course, The Unfinished Task*; and the inspiring article "No Reserves, No Retreats, No Regrets," by Howard Culbertson.

IVORY TOWERS AND TONGUES OF FIRE

WHAT GOLD CAN NEVER BUY

I heard Him call
"Come follow"
that was all.
My gold grew dim.
My soul went after Him.

—JOHN OXENHAM, FROM *BEES IN AMBER* (1913)

There is something so unsettling about the death of a young person, as if reality itself is somehow confused and the laws that govern life are operating against us rather than for us. What is especially remark-able about the death of William Borden, however, is that his friends and family interpreted his unusual life and the tragedy of his untimely death through another lens altogether. Of course they grieved, for Borden's life was lost in its very prime; he was only twenty-five. At the same time, though, they found peace—even *joy*—in the deep and con-fident assurance that Borden lived and died for something greater than this life alone.

"I do not want you to think of us as overwhelmed," Borden's mother wrote after burying her son's body in Egypt, "for we are not." Mrs. Borden and her daughter, Joyce, arrived in Cairo four hours after Wil-liam died. "God's loving care and mercy have been evident on every side," she continued in a letter written ten days after the funeral, "and it has been a real joy to be in the place where William, in those few short weeks, became so honored and loved, and was so *happy.*"

In faraway Kashmir, where one of Borden's friends from Yale, Sherwood Day, was serving as a missionary, the same sort of simple faith prevailed when news of Borden's death arrived. "Bill seems nearer and more gloriously living than he did at Yale or Cairo," young Sherwood wrote. "I cannot put on paper what his change of field means to me. He is the first of my friends whom I really loved, to be in that Other Place, and it makes that place very real. . . . I have no feeling of a life cut short," he concluded, "A life abandoned to Christ cannot be cut short."

As the story of William Borden continued to spread, so too did the global effect of his consecrated life. A brief booklet that told his story was printed in English and Arabic, Persian and Hindi, Dutch and Chinese. John Mott of the Student Volunteer Movement reported that Borden's example had more influence at their summer gatherings in 1913 than anything else. In fact, even among those who did not believe in Jesus, the story of William Borden and his sacrificial surrender inspired such genuine soul-searching regarding what is truly important in this life that one man, after reading a newspaper article about him, cried aloud in response, "I cannot understand it! There is no accounting for such a life."

For those who knew Borden best, though, the "accounting" for his life was obvious. During his student days at Yale, he and his friends discovered a depth of discipleship and life in God that even death itself could not conquer. Although the story of William Borden is fairly well known, the story of the wider student awakening that was taking place during his university years, of which Borden's Bible and prayer movement at Yale was just one part, is less familiar.

In 1905, the year that Bill Borden and Charley Campbell started praying together before breakfast, a periodical reported about what was happening not only at Yale but at multiple campuses across the country: "Never before in the history of universities have there been so many genuine spiritual awakenings among students." One of the reasons for the escalating momentum on campus was a Universal Day of Prayer for Students that had been called by John Mott and others for February 12, 1905. Numerous colleges and universities responded to the call, and it became a significant turning point in campus life. The Day of Prayer for Students in 1905 was not randomly selected, however, but was connected to a wider work of global awakening that started in Wales in 1904.

FROM WALES TO THE WORLD

I felt ablaze with a desire to go through the length and breadth of Wales to tell of the Savior. . . . I was willing to pay God for doing so.

—EVAN ROBERTS

While the movement at Yale might be traced to the early-morning prayer and Bible study led by William Borden, the privileged son of an American millionaire, the central figure in the 1904 awakening in Wales, a movement of truly global proportions, was a twenty-six-year-old student named Evan Roberts, the son of a Welsh coalminer. Evan left school at age eleven and worked in the mines with his father for more than a decade. Convinced his nation was in dire need of spiritual transformation, he returned to school in his mid-twenties to pursue an education in theology.

In September 1904, early in his studies, Roberts heard minister Seth Joshua pray aloud in Welsh, "Plyg ni, O Arglwydd," which is translated, "Bend us, O Lord." Desperate for a closer walk with God, Evan Roberts cried out in response, "Bend *me*, O Lord!" Shortly later, in the same meeting, Roberts experienced what he described as a baptism of the Holy Spirit: "I fell on my knees with my arms over the seat in front of me," he explained, "and the tears freely flowed."

Two months later, Evan Roberts returned to his hometown and told his story. Young people especially responded to his testimony at first, but soon, according to Jessie Penn-Lewis, who witnessed the awakening, "The whole community was shaken. Meetings lasted until four in the morning," she explained. "[H]undreds of colliers and tinplate workers were transformed. The men went straight to chapel from the mills." Remarkably, within six months the Welsh Revival resulted in more than one hundred thousand people deciding to following Jesus.

The effect of the national awakening produced striking social transformation as well as supernatural phenomena. Among the coal miners, harsh profanity was so radically diminished that there were reports of pit ponies needing to be retrained, apparently because the animals were unaccustomed to being treated with such kindness. In several places, local judges were presented with white gloves, as there were no crimes to be tried. In the region of Cardiganshire, an Anglican vicar distinctly heard the sound of singing in the air, as if the atmosphere itself was somehow charged with the presence of God. In another instance of phenomena and song, a young woman was converted in a meeting as she listened to the performance of a soloist in French, although the rest of the congregation was hearing the same song in their native Welsh.

What started as a local movement in Wales soon became a global trend of prayer and transformation as stories of the awakening spread. Similar instances of revival occurred in England, Scotland, Ireland, Germany, Australia, New Zealand, China, Japan, India and Korea. In the United States, college and university campuses were especially impacted. Reports of student conversions flowed in from Cornell and Rutgers, Mississippi State and Baylor, Stanford and Trinity, as well as numerous other campuses across the country.

One of the most measurable results of the 1905 awakening in collegiate life came in the form of the honor system being widely adopted in college examinations. "[Because] of the recognition of a higher code of ethics prevailing in student societies" explains Dr. Orr in *Campus Aflame*, "several prominent universities now deemed the *honor system* practicable." During this dynamic period figures like William Borden emerged at Yale, and E. Stanley Jones, who became a famous missionary to India and close friend of Mohandas Gandhi, studied at Asbury. But not only academic communities in America were affected by the awakening; startling testimonies of tongues of fire were soon reported from a place in California known as Azusa Street.

THE COMFORTER HAS COME

The entire room fell to their knees as fires of baptism
ignited spontaneously among them. Joy. Chaos. Beauty.
Sounds. Songs. Nothing could be defined, but everything
could be felt.

—CRAIG BORLASE

In early April of 1906, a few days before a violent earthquake shook San Francisco with such force that portions of the city were literally flattened by the impact, another sort of tremor—one of a decidedly spiritual nature—took place in Los Angeles. The epicenter of this spiritual awakening was neither a college campus nor did it primarily impact students at its start. Given time, though, the movement born during those influential days in 1906 affected people in *every* sphere of society, campuses included. It was not long before the exciting and controversial events that occurred at the turn of the twentieth century on Azusa Street in Los Angeles were multiplied around the world through a new and powerful expression of Christianity called Pentecostalism.

As early as June 1905 there was correspondence between Evan Roberts in Wales and Frank Bartleman, an American minister in California, about the potential of something taking place in California akin to what was taking place in Wales. Bartleman, it must be understood, was certainly not alone in his expectation. Stirring stories about the Welsh Revival had already fanned the flame of prayer and expectancy on multiple college campuses as well as in various denominations. John Mott and the SVM network reported positively on the movement, and leaders among Episcopalians, Baptists, Methodists, Lutherans and Presbyterians reported the same. Summing up the expectation most succinctly, one Presbyterian paper said: "the land seems to be on the lookout for a great outpouring of the Holy Spirit."

When the "outpouring" touched down in California, however, it broke every conceivable box of social and religious expectation. For starters, the most visible leader of the Azusa Street awakening was a decidedly humble, one-eyed African American named William Seymour. Second, the most noticeable markers of the movement were speaking in tongues and praying for miraculous healings, phenomena that most traditional denominations knew very little about. Finally, the controversial outpouring seriously challenged racial and social stereotypes by eagerly welcoming both blacks and whites, rich and poor into its meetings. In the memorable words of Rev. Bartleman (who was a poor, white preacher, by the way): "The color line was washed away at Azusa." And "[The] rich and educated were the same as the poor and ignorant."

Craig Borlase, in his insightful biography about William Seymour, has captured the stunning effect of the turning point meeting of the 1906 awakening at Azusa Street:

> Some were crying, some dancing. . . . [A]ll were feeling the intensity of a personal encounter with the Holy Spirit. The servant girl from across the street, Jennie Evans Moore . . . approached the dark wood piano, lifted the lid, and played a simple melody, . . . harmonized with simple chords given greater depth and tone by her pure voice. She sang out in French first of all, then in other languages. . . . Interpretations came from all over, each one reflecting the theme of God's glory and the power of His presence.

The unusual episode with Jennie Moore was shocking on multiples levels. For not only had the servant girl never been taught to play the piano, neither did she know French or any of the other languages in which she sang. In the days and weeks that followed, speaking in tongues—both known and unknown languages—increasingly became the identifying sign of the supernatural outpouring at Azusa Street.

For the modern critic, such phenomena might easily be dismissed as an intoxicating blend of spiritual hysteria and exaggerated religious reporting. (For the record, I believe it actually happened.) What is not so easily dismissed, however, is the global movement that resulted from Azusa Street. As recently as 2002, Professor David Martin of the

London School of Economics, who is an expert on global Pentecostalism, estimated that the members of churches and movements associated with the effects of Azusa Street now number more than 250 million people worldwide. Regardless of our opinions about the supernatural, *something* extraordinary clearly happened in 1906, and apparently that *something* is still happening today.

As has been the case from the fiery beginnings of Pentecostalism, the poor and marginalized remain the white-hot center of the movement, even though the rich and powerful are always welcome.

It is important to point out the unusual journey that has brought us thus far: from the story of a wealthy, white kid at Yale in 1905 to the Pentecostal movement of a poor, black preacher in 1906. Surely there is significance in the historical intersect of William Borden and William Seymour, and surely the different expressions of faith they represent have something to learn from one another.

A TALE OF TWO WILLIAMS

Is it possible to draw these extremes together . . . for
an intellectually robust, Biblically grounded, socially
engaged, expression of Christianity that is also
passionate about discipleship and comfortable in the
gifts of the Holy Spirit, marrying the contemplative
disciplines with the [passionate] and mystical practices
of the charismatics?

—PETE GREIG

William Borden and William Seymour both followed Jesus, but their journeys of faith led them in different directions in their understanding of the Holy Spirit. While Borden's work at Yale was clearly marked by biblical discipleship, in some ways it lacked the extraordinary power of Seymour's Pentecostal faith. The movement at Azusa Street, on the other hand, was especially well known for its miraculous power, particularly in the areas of speaking in tongues and healing the sick, but Seymour's movement was also known for its emotionalism and a tendency to rely on special revelation instead of deep and practical biblical teaching.

Although it was very rare, there are historical examples of these two movements making an effort to learn from each other in their earliest days. In 1906, for instance, Cecil Polhill-Turner, a member of the Cambridge Seven, sought a deeper filling of the Holy Spirit by visiting Azusa Street. Polhill-Turner, though not specifically from Borden's prayer and Bible movement at Yale, was certainly of a similar sort of social and faith background. One of the results of Polhill-Turner's visit to Azusa was the founding of the Pentecostal Missionary Union in 1909.

For the most part, though, the divergent streams of faith represented by Borden and Seymour learned very little from one another at the turn of the twentieth century. They lived and worshiped in different circles, distantly united by their common belief in Jesus, but worlds apart in the practice of their faith. We cannot help but wonder what might have happened had William Borden and William Seymour intentionally sought each other out, had the biblical depth of the movement at Yale and the Pentecostal power of Azusa Street humbly met in a mutual friendship of faith.

While the two Williams of our story never had the chance for such friendship, the modern expressions of Christianity they represent still do. The simple truth is that William Borden and William Seymour needed one another. Neither of them held the whole truth about God, and both had vital areas in which to grow. Indeed, one of the most beautiful facets of the worldwide Christian faith is that a rich, committed, Christ-centered kid like William Borden and a poor, empowered, Spirit-filled preacher like William Seymour have something to learn from one another.

The Holy Spirit is much more than a mysterious power, as evidenced in Seymour, or the hidden source of a truly surrendered life, as witnessed in Borden. The Holy Spirit is God, eternally one with the Father and Son. Jesus said the Holy Spirit would comfort and convict us, transform and empower us, enable and affirm us to be nothing less than friends of God, beloved children entrusted with the living authority of heaven (see John 14–16; Acts 1–2; Romans 8). If that is the full promise of the Holy Spirit's presence, then why do we settle for only a part?

FINDING YOUR PLACE IN HISTORY

Change, cleanse, use me as Thou shalt choose.
I take the full power of Thy Holy Spirit.

—WILLIAM BORDEN

He kept on, alone, and in response to his last prayer, a
sphere of white hot brilliance seemed to appear, draw
near, and fall on him. Divine love melted his heart.

—DOUGLAS NELSON, DESCRIBING THE AZUSA
EXPERIENCE OF WILLIAM SEYMOUR

Walking with God is a privilege that gold can never buy. William Borden of Yale knew that, as did William Seymour of Azusa Street. The essential takeaway of this chapter is pondering the profound lessons of *both* their lives. One of the most urgent needs of our generation is a deeper and healthier, more holistic and more powerful relationship with the Holy Spirit: a relationship rooted in a biblical understanding of God, a relationship not afraid of using common-sense when seeking for and operating in the charismatic gifts of the Holy Spirit, a relationship truly impassioned in its pursuit of being continually filled with the living and powerful presence of Jesus.

1. If you more easily identify with William Borden's background of faith, make it a point to humbly learn from someone whose experience of following Jesus is more like William Seymour's.

2. If you more easily identify with William Seymour's background of faith, make it a point to humbly learn from someone whose experi-

ence of following Jesus is more like William Borden's.

3. Never take yourself too seriously in this journey. One way to keep laughing through the various ups-and-downs in your pursuit of God is by keeping in mind that a man with the last name Seymour (pronounced: See-More) was actually blind in one eye.

INTERLUDE

Reflections on Student Movements

Since Jesus' time numberless bands of Christian youth have "turned the world upside down" and thus led [humanity] forward in its struggle for freedom and deeper religious experience. The universities have always been breeding places for such groups. Sometimes these groups have been by-products of the teaching of the university. Quite as frequently, however, they have been revolts against the restrictions on religious freedom and adventure that the university, along with the rest of society, placed upon youth.

—CLARENCE P. SHEDD

The year 1886 was significant in student history for two very different reasons. At Harvard, America's original college, chapel attendance was no longer required of the student body for the first time in 250 years. While Christian faith was never obligatory at Harvard and nontraditional theologies were welcomed on campus from very early in its history, chapel services had been part of the overall educational vision offered by this pioneering institution ever since it was founded in 1636. When compulsory chapel ceased at Harvard in 1886, a spiritual practice on campus that spanned a quarter of a millennium came to an end.

In a fascinating coincidence of history, it was also in 1886 that 251 college students from eighty-six campuses gathered in Northfield, Massachusetts, for the historic Mount Hermon Bible Conference with D. L. Moody. Chapter six tells the story of what happened at the Mount Hermon gathering and how the Student Volunteer Movement, which ultimately mobilized more than one hundred thousand student volunteers, was born during those momentous summer days. The important thing to recognize is that even as a *compulsory* form of student faith was fading at Harvard, a *voluntary* movement of student mission was emerging at Mount Hermon.

The shift at Harvard in 1886 was part of a much larger shift in education that was transforming American colleges and universities throughout this time. In *The Soul of the American University*, George Marsden explains that by "the 1920s the evangelical Protestantism of the old-time colleges had been effectively excluded from leading university classrooms." Older traditions of theology were systematically replaced with new and innovative ideas in scientific reasoning. Whereas before *character development* had been a primary aim of Christian higher education, in the new and increasingly secular climate, *cutting-edge research* now took precedence over most everything else.

The responses to these changes were varied. Some educators and students openly abandoned their time-honored traditions of faith and wholeheartedly embraced the rapid developments in modern thought. Others sought compromise between the two positions, denying certain portions of the Bible, such as the deity of Jesus, for instance, while still holding on to the overall moral teachings of Christianity. Other groups challenged the secular developments in education by insisting on a reading of the Bible that held fast to the "fundamentals" of the faith.

It is important for us to understand these various responses to Christianity and education because it was during this defining period in collegiate history that voluntary student movements like the college YMCA and the SVM were most active. In many ways they were filling the spiritual void that appeared on campuses when colleges and universities began to systematically move away from their faith foundations.

These voluntary student movements, however, were by no means unaffected by the profound changes in education that were taking place scientifically and theologically. It can be argued, in fact, that it was precisely because of such changes that the YMCA began to drift from its early evangelistic focus, so much so that it is hardly known as a force for evangelism today. A similar history of decline affected the once mighty SVM, which voted itself out of existence as its numbers and focus began to gradually fade.

As the strength of the SVM was visibly waning throughout the 1920s and 1930s, and a steady wave of secularization was transforming colleges and universities across the country, followers of Jesus on campus began pioneering new initiatives of faith. At a student Bible conference in the summer of 1936, for example, the Student Foreign Missions Fellowship (SFMF) was launched to reengage students with the call of global mission. Local SFMF chapters began to rapidly multiply on campuses across the country, and by autumn 1941 there were 36 chapters with 2,628 student members.

In 1945, SFMF joined forces with the InterVarsity Christian Fellowship (IVCF), a movement that came to the United States from Canada in 1939, but that traced its origins all the way back to a group of student believers at the University of Cambridge, England, in 1877. From its earliest years of development in the United States, IVCF was committed to being an ongoing evangelizing presence *in the university*, as opposed to an evangelistic outreach *to the university.* "IVCF was a student mission," explains Keith and Gladys Hunt in a historical account of the first fifty years of the movement, "not a mission to students. The campus was not a fishing pond for converts," they continue, "IVCF was not a group of people making forays onto the campus; it was an evangelizing fellowship *within* the university."

Because InterVarsity viewed their campus initiatives as lasting communities of scholarship and evangelistic faith rather than as temporary projects for quick conversion, the movement was well received on "secular" campuses even when faculty members and unbelieving students disagreed with them. "I do not agree with Inter-Varsity in its theology" confessed a professor at a conference on religion at a state university:

> But there is one thing that does appeal. This movement is not working from the outside like a propaganda agency trying to tell students what they should believe or what they should do. Rather, this is a genuine grass-roots student movement, a genuine expression of [student] feeling and conviction. We may not agree with your viewpoint, but we will defend your right to carry on a work when it is done on this basis.

As IVCF continued its steady growth on campuses, the movement received an important surge of encouragement in the post-World War II era by partnering with The Navigators (NAV), a ministry started in 1931 by a young Californian named Dawson Trotman. The work was especially focused on helping high school students become effective disciples of Jesus. As the ministry grew throughout the late 1930s and early 1940s, NAV soon directed its disciple-making emphasis toward the millions of soldiers involved in the war. When these servicemen returned to the United States and began to enter colleges and universities, the Navigators' leadership encouraged them to partner with existing student movements like InterVarsity, instead of starting new discipleship and evangelistic groups on campus.

In 1946, through the combined efforts of IVCF and SFMF, an international missions convention for students was held in Toronto. In a sense this gathering was "receiving the baton" from the Student Volunteer Movement conferences that had been so effective in mobilizing students toward global mission in an earlier era. The 1946 convention in Toronto only drew 575 students, but two years later when it was moved to a more central location at the University of Illinois campus at Champaign-Urbana, its numbers more than doubled.*

Attending the 1948 gathering at Urbana was Jim Elliot, a young man from Wheaton College. Elliot had long been focused on missionary service and was the leader of the SFMF chapter on his campus. During the Urbana convention in 1948, Elliot became convinced of something he had been praying about for an extended period. "The Lord has done what I wanted Him to do this week," he wrote after the convention, "as I analyze my feelings now, I feel quite at ease about saying that tribal work in South American jungles is the general direction of my missionary purpose."

Shortly after Jim Elliot graduated from Wheaton College in 1949, he wrote in his journal, "He is no fool who gives what he cannot keep to gain that which he cannot lose." Elliot was writing about his commitment to follow Jesus, regardless of what that commitment might cost. Six years later, while working in a remote region of Ecuador with the Huaorani people group, Elliot and four of his friends—Nate Saint, Roger Youderian, Ed McCulley and Pete Fleming—were speared to death. As the story of their lives and sacrifice spread, mission movements on campus exponentially increased.

In 1951, five years before Elliot and his friends were martyred, Bill Bright, a student at Fuller Theological Seminary, received an impression from God that he was to devote his life to leading students to Jesus. In response, Bright and his wife, Vonette, organized a twenty-four-hour prayer chain for students at the University of California at Los Angeles (UCLA). Within a few months, more than 250 UCLA students decided to follow Jesus, including the president of the student

---

*The IVCF student mission convention is now known as Urbana and continues to this day. Alongside Urbana, another significant student development that involved IVCF during the late 40s was the founding of the International Fellowship of Evangelical Students (IFES) in 1947. The IFES is a global collective of national student movements, currently representing student fellowships in 143 countries.

body, the editor of the campus newspaper and a number of well-known UCLA athletes.

At the advice of a professor friend from Fuller Seminary, the Brights named their new student initiative Campus Crusade for Christ (CC). The early growth of CC was nothing short of phenomenal, as evangelistic enthusiasm rapidly multiplied from UCLA to campuses across the country. During this time, Crusade's partnership with other student movements was essential, and it was not long before the national directors of InterVarsity, the Navigators and Campus Crusade were meeting with one another regularly to share vision, pray together and plan for the future.

A final movement that is broadly representative of this era in student history, especially as it relates to the momentum toward global mission on campus, is Youth With A Mission (YWAM), which was founded by Loren Cunningham in 1960. When Cunningham was a twenty-year-old college student at the Assemblies of God Bible College in Springfield, Missouri, he spent a portion of his summer break ministering with a gospel quartet in the Bahamas. During that short-term summer endeavor, Cunningham experienced a vision from God that revealed waves and waves of young people covering the nations of the earth with the message of Jesus.

As he pondered his vision and what it might mean, particularly concerning to Cunningham was the fact that so many college and university students seemed to start their studies with a passion to serve God as missionaries, but that by the time they completed their degrees, their commitment to such international service waned. After he graduated from college, Cunningham spent a period of time traveling around the world in an attempt to understand cultural diversity and the urgent needs of the global community. Shortly after he returned to America, the work of YWAM began. "It would be an organization," according to the early history of the movement, "that sent kids out after high school to gain a sense of purpose when going to college, and that welcomed all Christians no matter what the denomination."

The late 1960s and early 1970s were a transformative and volatile time on campus. Youth culture in general was experiencing the unpredictable effect of widespread cultural change. Part three of *God on Campus* begins by exploring various facets of the student transformation that took place during this period, and then connects that very recent history to the electrifying story of what is happening on campuses today. In the words of John W. Alexander (1918–2002), president of IVCF for seventeen years:

> God is at work on college campuses where he is building a portion of the body of Jesus Christ. Too often Christians write off the campus as hopelessly detached from God's presence and beyond the reach of the Holy Spirit. We repudiate this defeatist attitude and espouse the belief that even at the most hostile school, the principles in Habakkuk 1:15 apply: "Observe and be astounded, and be amazed; for I am doing a work in your day which you would not believe even if it were told you." God is the great active agent on these campuses; if he were not thus engaged, there would be little point to our efforts.

Part Three

LIVING FAITH

Prayer is the greatest force that we can wield.

It is the greatest talent which God has given

us. He has given it to every person. . . . We

may differ among ourselves as to wealth, as

to our social position, as to our [education],

as to our . . . ability, as to our inherited

characteristics; but in this matter of exercising

the greatest force that is at work in the world

today, we are on the same footing.

—JOHN MOTT

8

Columbia University, 1968. *Five days after Martin Luther King Jr. was assassinated in Memphis, Tennessee, several hundred students and faculty members gathered in St. Paul's Chapel to pay respect to his life and memory.*

King was the leading voice of the civil rights movement, a transcendent figure of hope who represented the possibility of healing in a time of tremendous social pain. When MLK was murdered, America's hopes of healing and dreams of racial harmony seemed to die with him.

Riots broke out in 168 towns and cities across the nation. There were 711 fires in Washington, D.C., alone. Federal troops mounted machine guns on the steps of the Capitol and soldiers of the Army's 3rd Infantry Division were stationed at the White House. Although order was eventually restored, it was an exceptionally tense time in America, and the campus of Columbia was no exception.

On April 9, David Truman, the vice president of the university, stepped to the microphone in St. Paul's Chapel to deliver a five-minute eulogy about King. The service was proceeding as planned until a junior named Mark Rudd, the leader of an activist group on campus called Students for a Democratic Society (SDS), rose from his seat and resolutely walked to the platform.

Stepping in front of the vice president, Rudd positioned himself at the microphone and calmly faced the congregation. "Dr. Truman and President Kirk are committing a moral outrage against the memory of Dr. King," the student said. Rudd then quietly but passionately outlined numerous ways that he deemed the administration of Columbia was failing to follow the visionary ideals of MLK, ranging from the university's vacillating stance on student protests against the Vietnam War to the administration's approval of a controversial building project in Harlem.

The junior stepped off the platform, walked down the center aisle and defiantly exited the building through the main doors of the chapel. As if on cue, forty students rose from their seats and followed him out the door.

Two weeks later, Rudd wrote an open letter to Grayson Kirk, the president of the university. "You might want to know," Rudd said in the letter, "what is wrong with this society, since, after all, you live in a very tight self-created world."

We can point to the war in Vietnam as an example of the unimaginable wars of aggression you are prepared to fight to maintain your control over your empire. . . . We can point to your using us as cannon fodder to fight your war. We can point out your mansion window to the ghetto below you've helped to create through your racist University expansion policies, through your unfair labor practices. . . . We can point to this University, your University, which trains us to be lawyers and engineers, and managers for your IBM, your Socony Mobil, your IDA [Institute for Defense Analyses] . . . or else to be scholars and teachers in more universities like this one. We can point, in short, to our own meaningless studies, our identity crises, and our revulsion with being cogs in your corporate machines as a product of and reaction to a basically sick society.

After a long and articulate litany of accusations, Mark Rudd wrapped up his revolutionary letter to the establishment by quoting a controversial African American poet. "Up against the wall, mother******," the concluding line of the letter stated, "this is a stick-up." On April 23, the day after Rudd's letter was made public, the angst at Columbia, which had been steadily building for some months, was unleashed.

The SDS, in partnership with another activist group called the Students' Afro-American Society (SAS), were leading a protest in the center of campus that day. The strategic aim of the demonstration was to create a black and white coalition, united in their efforts to force change at Columbia. Through a blur of rapidly unfolding events, however, which included a breakdown in communication and strategy between the SDS and SAS leadership, the demonstration quickly evolved into a very serious situation.

During the next six days, five buildings on campus were taken over in protest. The dean of Columbia and two other staff were held hostage. Outside activists became increasingly involved in the volatile demonstration. The president's office was commandeered and an iconic photograph of student David Shapiro—wearing sunglasses, smoking a cigar and sitting at President Kirk's desk—was released to the media.

When student groups that disagreed with the protestors stepped in to forcibly stop the mayhem, violence broke out and the NYPD was called in to handle the situation. In the early morning hours of April 30, hundreds of police officers descended on Columbia and cleared the five occupied buildings first, and then the campus as a whole.

"The Bust"—as it was called—was a brutal affair. Protestors were arrested, 695 in all, the majority of them students. According to hospital and departmental records, 92 demonstrators and 17 officers were injured. "There was great violence," reported the fact-finding commission appointed to investigate the crisis at Columbia after it was over. "Given the conditions on the campus," the report concluded, "violence was unavoidable."

As word about the uprising at Columbia spread, similar instances of student revolt broke out on other campuses. More than five hundred people rallied at Princeton and fifty students at Stony Brook staged a seventeen-hour sit-in as a show of solidarity with the demonstrators at Columbia. At Northwestern, the main business office and the dean of students' office were taken over by students in protest.

The late 1960s were not only a seedbed for revolution on campus; youth culture in general was being transformed. In the summer of 1969, Woodstock took place on a six-hundred-acre dairy farm in Bethel, New York. Half a million hippies, in search of a counterculture society, showed up for the four-day music and arts festival.

Fortunately, the historic concert was a peaceful event. During a similar show five months later in California, however, at a three-hundred-thousand-strong daylong gig called Altamont, four people were dead before the day was over. The overlap between musical expression and volatile uprising was pervasive: early-sixties folk rock like 1964's "The Times They Are a-Changin'" chronicled the emerging political consciousness and at the same time inspired it:

Come senators, congressmen
Please heed the call
Don't stand in the doorway
Don't block up the hall
For he that gets hurt
Will be he who has stalled
There's a battle outside
And it is ragin'.
It'll soon shake your windows
And rattle your walls
For the times they are a-changin'.

By the time 1968 came around, rock n' roll both encouraged the public angst, as in the Rolling Stones' "Street Fighting Man" ("The time is right for fighting in the street, boy") and sighed in exasperation at it, as with the Beatles' "Revolution": "You say you want a revolution. . . . Well, you know, we all want to change the world."

Somewhere in between the summer days of free love at Woodstock and the December tragedy at Altamont, six students at a small Methodist college in Wilmore, Kentucky, determined to experiment with another sort of countercultural revolution. Like most everybody else in the late 1960s, these students at Asbury College wanted change. But the way they went about such transformation was decidedly different than the mainstream movement of revolt.

Their plan was pretty basic. For thirty days, they would pray every morning. During the thirty minutes they allotted for prayer, they would read the Bible as well, especially paying attention to any areas of action the Scriptures called them to. In this simple way these six students, as best they knew how, sought transformation in their lives and on their campus. They called their plan The Great Experiment.

At the start of the winter term in 1970, the students expanded their *experiment. Each one asked six others to join them, making the total number involved thirty-six. The Great Experiment lasted throughout January, culminating in a chapel service in Hughes Auditorium on the last day of the month. During the service, according to a faculty member who was present that day, the thirty-six students reported about "what time with God had done" in their lives and invited others to join them.*

On February 3, the very next chapel service at Asbury, the dean of students, Custer Reynolds, opened the meeting by telling about his own spiritual journey. Reynolds then welcomed others to share their stories as well. A number of students immediately responded. They spoke with unusual conviction about what was happening in their lives, with one openly rebellious senior humbly confessing, "I'm not believing that I'm standing here . . . [but] last night the Holy Spirit flooded in and filled my life."

When the fifty minutes scheduled for chapel were coming to a close, a philosophy professor suggested that people might want to stay for a while longer to pray. It seemed like a wise proposal, so Dean Reynolds encouraged the students that the front of the chapel was open for prayer.

As soon as the invitation was given, a rush of students came forward. "They started pouring to the altar," the dean later explained, "[something] just broke." The bell sounded for classes, but nobody moved. Instead, students and professors began to quietly pray. Some even started to weep as they became acutely aware of God's presence.

When the chapel service was still going after twenty-four hours, the local and state media picked up the story. As the service continued, leading news outlets across the country began carrying reports as well. "I'm sick and tired of covering campus riots," one seasoned reporter explained, "If those kids run out of something to pray for about 2 o'clock in the morning, ask them to pray for me."

Unlike the uprising at Columbia, which was mainly marked by accusation, the movement at Asbury was especially marked by confession. In fact, the awakening was later described as a "spiritual phenomenon of integrity," as person after person humbly confessed specific areas of sin and failure in their lives, things that held them back from following Jesus and caring for others. During those unusual days at Asbury, it seemed as if sin was simply out of place. For 185 hours, the chapel service in Hughes Auditorium kept going. When a reporter finally approached the president of Asbury, Dennis Kinlaw, and asked him to explain what was happening, Kinlaw simply replied, "Well, you may not understand . . . but the only way I know how to account for this is that last Tuesday morning . . . Jesus walked into Hughes Auditorium, and He's been there ever since."*

---

*For more on the events at Columbia in 1968, see the Cox Commission Report, *Crisis at Columbia* and also Jerry L. Avorn, *Up Against the Ivy Wall: A History of the Columbia Crisis*. As it relates to the awakening at Asbury in 1970, see Robert E. Coleman, ed., *One Divine Moment*, as well as the personal account of Dennis Kinlaw, *A Revival Account: Asbury 1970* (DVD).

WHEN HISTORY IS RIPE FOR CHANGE

UPRISING AT COLUMBIA AND THE GREAT EXPERIMENT AT ASBURY

This vital decision rests with the . . . reform-minded students. They can save or destroy the institution.

—COX COMMISSION REPORT

Most people are dying for something to live for, and students are by no means an exception to this rule. As was the case at Columbia and Asbury, campuses are very often the places where our intrinsic ache for a meaningful purpose in life is first awakened. That burgeoning desire is expressed in both subtle and obvious ways in student life, whether that is bucking against the rules at a conservative college like Wheaton in Illinois or attending class *sans* clothes at a liberal university like Berkeley in California.

Inspired by the true-life story of the 1990s "Naked Guy" at Berkeley, a friend of mine wrote a satirical song called "Uncle Milo's Nudist Farm." It recounts the bizarre story of a college student named Tommy who strips down to his birthday suit and tells his friend Fred, "I can't stand the pressure to act this same old play. I'm sick of being normal," he explains, "I think I've lost my way." Now, the story is obviously intended to be humorous, with memorable images of

Tommy and Fred in "just shoes and backpacks." At the same time, though, the song packs a poignant ending when Tommy quietly confesses: "I cried out to the people, 'Help me if you can!' I looked for something real," he says to his friend, "but no one answered my demand."

In a 2006 obituary about Andrew Martinez, the real-life "Naked Guy" at Berkeley, the *New York Times* reported, "It was easy to dismiss his behavior as a silly stunt, but to those who knew him, Martinez was guided by an endearing, if naive, sort of . . . idealism." The idealism of Martinez did not last, however, as he was dismissed from the university in 1992 and diagnosed with a mental illness shortly later. Embittered and disillusioned, it was not long before Berkeley's Naked Guy was piling rocks in the center of busy intersections in preparation for what he described as a *coming revolution*.

In 1968, the year of the crisis at Columbia, it seemed as if most college students were on the lookout for a *coming revolution*. America was in the middle of an unpopular war in Vietnam. Martin Luther King Jr. and Bobby Kennedy were assassinated within nine weeks of one another. Angry students in France, furious with their university system and disillusioned with social norms, took to the streets in Paris and sparked a national strike. Student riots in Mexico City resulted in some two hundred people being shot and killed during a brutal government crackdown. In the words of Lance Morrow, a professor at Boston University, "Nineteen sixty-eight had the vibrations of an earthquake about it. . . . [Like] a knife blade that severed past from future."

It was a time in which history itself was ripe for change. In the language of the New Testament, such periods are referred to in terms of *kairos*, a Greek word that means the *fullness of time*. According to the Gospel narratives and the letters of Paul, it was during such an era that Jesus walked the earth and the Christian movement was born. The concept of *kairos* suggests there are particular seasons of history that are somehow pregnant with potential. For better or worse, the sixties were just such a time, and one way or another, change was coming.

KAIROS CAN GO EITHER WAY

Those of you who are black can be filled with hatred, with bitterness and a desire for revenge. We can move toward further polarization. Or we can make an effort, as Dr. King did, to understand, to reconcile ourselves and to love. . . . Violence breeds violence, repression brings retaliation, and only a cleansing of our whole society can remove this sickness from our soul.

—BOBBY KENNEDY

Bobby Kennedy was campaigning in Indianapolis the day Martin Luther King Jr. was assassinated. He was scheduled to address a large rally of African Americans, but his aides begged him not to and the local police advised against the gathering as well. Racial relations were just too fragile, they argued, and riots in other cities were already beginning to take place. Kennedy addressed the crowd anyway. Breaking the news of King's death to the stunned gathering, the speech Kennedy gave that day was historic, humbly articulating the need for racial reconciliation and urging the devastated crowd toward a peaceful response. Notably, Indianapolis was one of the few major cities in America that did not experience rioting in the aftermath of King's death.

Tragically, however, Bobby Kennedy was assassinated just nine weeks later. That's the volatile thing about *kairos*. When history arrives at a *fullness of time*, it can go either way, toward violence on the one side or love on the other. As to which way *kairos* goes in any given situation, one of the determining factors is whether people choose to live by arrogance or humility, accusation or confession.

It is especially important to see this principle at work in the cases of Columbia and Asbury. The uprising at Columbia, while accomplishing the goal of halting the building project in Harlem, seriously failed in

the larger value that was behind that goal, which was to create a black
and white coalition on campus. Because the movement was so thoroughly rooted in accusation, it meant that there was always someone
else to blame and little room for constructive healing in the critical
area of racial reconciliation. As a result, when the campus takeover
actually took place, black students controlled one building and white
students controlled the others.

Mark Rudd's revolutionary letter to the administration, which was
the proverbial straw that broke the camel's back in the case of the crisis at Columbia, was brilliantly articulated but dripping with cynicism
and accusation. It should be no wonder, then, that as the movement
grew, even more accusation followed as student groups quickly turned
on one another. At Asbury, on the other hand, the Great Experiment
created an environment of expectation not dependent on someone
else changing. Thus, as the movement grew there, the critical mark of
the awakening was not pointing the finger at another but allowing
God to search your own heart instead.

The effect of such humility in action was remarkable, resulting in
both racial and generational healing. "In such a spirit of love," wrote
one of the observers of the awakening at Asbury, "whether it is on a
college or university campus, in a church or community, in government or the nation, reconciliation follows."

> Grudges are gone, prejudices forgotten. Many a person rose
> from the altar [at Asbury] with a new attitude toward racial prob-
> lems. Black and white stood side by side and shared their sav-
> ior's love. Divisions were healed between faculty and student.
> Even the generation gap seemed to evaporate. One eighty-year-
> old grandmother expressed the secret pretty well when she tes-
> tified like a teenager, "I'm high on Jesus."

Now that certainly does not mean we should only focus on personal issues and thereby expect social transformation to naturally follow. But it does mean that we cannot expect others to change if we
have not experienced change ourselves.

CONFESSION AND FREEDOM

Utter honesty has been the standard. From the beginning, persons have laid their hearts bare. Unashamed of new-found peace with God, they have shared pointedly what their difficulties have been and what Jesus Christ has done to bring about a transformation.

—ARTHUR L. LINDSAY, COMMENTING ON
THE ASBURY REVIVAL

One of the great strengths of the Catholic tradition is the practice of confession. Protestant-background believers have historically been hesitant about ongoing rhythms of confession out of fear that talking to a priest about sin may substitute for talking with God. What is striking about times of revival, however, is that even among Protestants, confession becomes the norm. This is particularly true in collegiate history. "Besides unusual prayer and preaching and extraordinary conviction of wrong-doing," explains J. Edwin Orr in *Campus Aflame*, "the outstanding and inevitable mark of the college awakenings has been confession of sin."

There is something about the presence of Jesus that makes sin seem out of place. It is not as if people are unmercifully condemned or accused in such times, for on the contrary, Jesus was known as a *friend of sinners*. In times of awakening, though, the façade of sin is exposed, evil is revealed for what it really is, and the journey of freedom begins by way of confession.

"I need help," a young woman said to Dr. Kinlaw during the revival at Asbury, "I'm a liar. I lie so much I don't know when I'm lying. . . . [W]hat do I do?" she asked. Years later, Kinlaw recounted the story of his encounter with the distraught and humble student:

> Well I sat there for a moment or two, and I had never said this to anybody else, but I looked at her and I said, "Why don't you start

back to the last person you remember that you lied to. Confess it to that person, and ask him or her to forgive you."

"Oh," she said, "that would kill me."

I said, "No, it would probably cure you."

Three days later, she came to me radiant, and she said, "Dr. Kinlaw, I'm free." I said, "what do you mean, you're free?" She said, "I just hit my 34th person and I'm free."

That sort of bold confession, it should be understood, was not limited to students alone during the Asbury awakening. "I have been keeping up the outward appearances," confessed a psychology professor to the entire student body, "but there has been no peace or joy in my life. It has been dry," he said, "I can't go on like this." Two days later, having humbly acknowledged his brokenness and encountering God in the process, the same professor addressed the students again and spoke of a "new purpose for living."

Even among the skeptics at Asbury in 1970, those especially wary of emotional religious meetings, the awakening still had powerful effect. "There came that critical moment when I was forced to admit," explained one such student, "that my self-sufficiency was failing me. . . . I prayed at the altar for an hour and a half, not shedding a tear, but undergoing a spiritual revitalization that has revolutionized my life."

As students and professors honestly dealt with their disappointment and shame, patterns of sin and spiritual hypocrisy, the Asbury awakening spread to other campuses. Each weekend, traveling teams of students would tell the stories of what was happening at Asbury in multiple churches, youth groups, colleges and universities across the nation. By the summer of 1970 the revival had multiplied to more than 130 campuses. It was an extraordinary season of collegiate prayer and confession, and was part of a larger movement of spiritual transformation that seemed like it was on the very edge of becoming a nationwide awakening.

THE JESUS MOVEMENT

*Jesus freaks. Evangelical hippies. Or, as many prefer to
be called, street Christians. Under different names—and
in rapidly increasing numbers—they are the latest
incarnation of that oldest of Christian phenomena:
footloose, passionate bearers of the Word, preaching the
kingdom of heaven among the dispossessed of the earth.*

—*TIME*, AUGUST 3, 1970

While the revival at Asbury mostly affected straight-laced students and cleancut professors, there was a wider work of faith emerging among the fringe elements of society. It was called The Jesus Movement. Disillusioned by violent uprisings like what happened at Columbia and burned by the emptiness they experienced when their experiential drugs wore off, young people by the thousands began following Jesus in the late sixties and early seventies. "I felt the hip scene was filled with plastic love and plastic peace," explained David Hoyt, one of the movement's early leaders, in a 1970 interview with *Time* magazine, "Their love was lust and their peace was a finger sign."

These hippies wanted something deeper than what the typical counterculture was offering. When many of them found Jesus, a flood of unique ministries and communes were born. Jesus-centered coffeehouses were particularly popular during this period, and a wave of new music resulted from the movement as well. Edgy Christian musicians like Larry Norman pioneered a new genre of music that combined the rhythms of rock 'n' roll with the traditional tenets of the faith.

The Jesus Movement on campus came in various and fascinatingly colorful forms. In 1969, for instance, the Christian World Liberation Front (CWLF) was founded on the radical campus of Berkeley. The leader of CWLF, which was best known for its underground paper *Right On*, was Jack Sparks, a former Penn State professor.

When radicals of a different perspective dubbed the CWLF as "Jesus Freaks," the group claimed the derogatory title as a badge of honor, and before long it was attached to the Jesus Movement as a whole.

In June 1972, Campus Crusade hosted a major evangelism event in Dallas that gathered eighty thousand people, representing every state in America and sixty-eight nations. The gathering was called Explo '72. It made the cover of *Life* magazine and brought together on stage figures like Billy Graham and Johnny and June Cash. The final day of Explo '72 was an eight-hour music festival that packed some 150,000 people into the Cotton Bowl. Because rock 'n' roll was involved and also because Explo '72 was broadly ecumenical, working with Protestant and Roman Catholic ministries alike, many conservative groups and churches were critical of the historic event.

In some ways the weeklong story of Explo '72 reflects the sum story of the Jesus Movement altogether. Its dynamism was just a little too explosive for traditional churches. "Much of the heat of the Jesus Movement," explain revival historians Malcolm McDow and Alvin Reid in their book *Firefall*, "was lost before it greatly affected the denominations." Many churches were unwilling to embrace the uniqueness of the movement, and many within the movement were unwilling to embrace the churches. As a result, the Jesus Movement was stunted in its growth and did not become the nationwide awakening that many hoped it would be.

Simultaneously, though, we must keep in mind that genuine transformation takes time. Martin Luther King Jr. was assassinated in 1968, but forty years later Barack Obama was elected as the first African American president of the United States. In the same way, could it be that there is still more to come from the Jesus Movement of the sixties and seventies and the awakening at Asbury in 1970? For we must never forget that even when history itself is ripe for change, lasting transformation still takes time.

FINDING YOUR PLACE IN HISTORY

I had no idea that history was being made.
I was just tired of giving in.

—ROSA PARKS

One of the best ways we can respond to the *kairos* of our own era is by choosing to be marked by confession instead of accusation. Rather than merely adding more words to the angry arguments surrounding the culture wars of our generation—arguments which at times sound suspiciously like a "noisy gong or a clanging symbol" (see 1 Corinthians 13:1)—perhaps we would do better to first humble ourselves in prayer and confession before we begin pointing a finger in judgment. As a practical measure of whether your life is marked by confession or accusation, ask yourself this question: *Am I known more by what I am for or by what I am against?*

1. Consider creating your own Great Experiment, tailor-made for your campus, and ask a few of your friends to join you in the journey.

2. Keep in mind that when it comes to confession and freedom, J. Edwin Orr advised: "Let the circle of the offense be the circle of the confession made. In other words, secret sins should always be secretly confessed, private sins should be privately confessed, and open sins should be openly confessed."

Central Ohio, 2007. *When legendary Amish barn builder Josie Miller was brought in by Liberty Presbyterian Church to help construct a sanctuary for their congregation in 1994, the seventy-five-year-old Amish patriarch probably had no idea that the sacred barn he was building would one day become part of the unfolding spiritual history of campuses in America.*

Whether Miller knew that student history was in the making or not, however, the massive "Barn Church" he helped design was definitely built to last. Its huge supporting beams each measure more than a foot in diameter, with the largest timber girder weighing a solid 3,100 pounds. The Barn Church is so sturdily built, in fact, that experts estimate the building will still be standing in five hundred years.

Just thirteen years after its construction, seventy-two students from eleven campuses gathered in the famous Barn Church on March 31, 2007, to tell stories about what God was doing in their lives. They talked and prayed for hours, and before the evening was over, they knelt down together on the smooth hickory floors of the sacred barn and officially launched forty days of nonstop student prayer across the Buckeye State. They called their initiative "Campus Ohio."

Allison Brooks, a graduate of Ohio State University, together with Molly Gibson of Miami University and a few other friends helped initiate and network this surge of statewide, collegiate prayer. Their plan was simple: forty days of 24/7 prayer, passed like a baton from one campus to another, seamlessly connecting students across Ohio in a chain of nonstop intercession.

"[Although] the university students participating in the forty days of prayer . . . hail from all over the state," reported an online periodical that covered the 2007 initiative, "they are putting geography and rivalry aside to worship and pray and move together. From Xavier, to Bowling Green, to Ohio State, to the University of Cincinnati and be-

yond," the article continues, "these students are joining together as one people, one body, one campus. Campus Ohio."

In the early autumn of 2002, Allison Brooks was a freshman at Columbus State Community College, paying her way through school by working a part-time job at a local mall. Sometime during that fall she decided to read the Gospel of Matthew.

Even though Allison had known the story of Jesus since she was a child, there was something about the Gospel that seemed different to her when she read it this time. The words were all the same, but the central character had somehow become more real. "I was captivated by his conversations," Allison later explained, "how Jesus spent time with people. I wanted to be like him, to talk like him, to treat others like [he did]. I was so hungry to know Jesus that I wanted to eat my Bible!"

As Allison's fascination with Jesus grew, so did her sense of bewilderment and wonder, confusion and even frustration regarding one area of his life. "I was annoyed by the prayer life of Jesus," she confessed. "[M]y experience told me prayer was what happened before meals, or in a moment of tragedy or panic, but I saw something different in Jesus."

What especially struck Allison was the frequency with which Jesus prayed, and the natural way he went about it, as if an open conversation with God or spending an entire night in prayer was a completely normal thing to do. She came away from her reading of the Gospel convinced that prayer was the central "thing" in Jesus' life that made him tick, the open secret of his unusual communion with the One he called Father.

From that time forward, Allison began to "experiment" in prayer. She prayed by herself. She wrote her prayers down. She even took the risk of praying out loud with her friends, something she had been very nervous to do, and discovered the realness and freedom in prayer that came when it was not about "praying to others, but to God."

As Allison's confidence in prayer increased, her adventures in faith did too. She was no longer afraid to tell people about what was happening in her life and she began to ache for others to know a similar *sort of friendship with God. Throughout the next year, while she prayed for her friends and coworkers, Allison learned to not give up in prayer even when it seemed like things would never change. As she held on in faith, four of her friends, two housemates and two coworkers (including her boss), decided to follow Jesus.*

During this time a number of Allison's journal entries begin recording conversations and prayers about a "campus-wide prayer thing." By this point, Allison had made plans to transfer from the community college where she was attending to Ohio State University (OSU), the most populated campus in the country. Her journal entries about the "campus-wide prayer thing" were in reference to OSU. It was an idea she and a close friend from Campus Crusade, Katie Jones, had been talking together and praying about for some time:

> *Katie and I prayed time and time again for something swirling in our hearts and minds along the lines of prayer and unity. I referred to it in my journal as "this campus-wide prayer thing.". . .*
>
> *We weren't sure what God was leading into as far as what this was going to look like, but we did dream of what things could be like if we prayed . . . and we knew that He was leading. We knew this increasing desire in our hearts was not of ourselves but a desire deposit[ed] from God. When we prayed, the desire grew.*
>
> *It wasn't really intentional on our end . . . except that we had experienced the power of prayer and the intimate friendship we can know and experience with God in and through prayer. Our lives were turned upside down by this discovery, and we wanted the Church at Ohio State to get caught with it . . . and the campus [to] be immersed [in] this reality.*

Through an unusual chain of events that helped her know she was on the right track, and with the help of some humble leaders from a local church, Allison started something called Love OSU in October of 2004. The central aim of Love OSU, which is still operating at Ohio State, is to help students come together and pray for their campus. "Our vision is . . . Jesus: obsessively, dangerously, and undeniably

Jesus," their website plainly states, borrowing the words from "The Vision," a poem by Pete Greig.

In the early days of Love OSU, what that vision looked like practically was gathering students to pray every two weeks and encouraging them to embrace the spiritual discipline of fasting on the first Monday of each month. The goal was not to start a new organization but to strengthen existing campus ministries by helping their students learn how to pray.

As the momentum in prayer steadily began to grow at Ohio State, one of the most important side effects was the fostering of unity. Students from multiple ministries were getting to know one another for the first time. That sort of friendship first, relational dynamic quickly became a defining trait for the evolving work of Love OSU. In the words of Allison, "The church [was] everywhere, we just [didn't] know each other!"

Throughout the next two years, as the story of Love OSU continued to unfold, Allison and her friends at Ohio State came in contact with a number of national works who helped them in their development, including Campus Renewal Ministries, 24-7 Prayer, Campus Church Networks and Burning Heart Ministries. The momentum was building rapidly now, and it seemed clear that God was creating something that would not only impact OSU but that might in fact influence campuses across the country.

Allison had been completely transformed through her simple "experiment" in prayer. The young woman who was once nervous about praying in front of her friends had since discovered such boldness in God that she was now lovingly known as "Crazy Allison" across campus.

Before long, Love OSU began renting a house within walking distance of Ohio State, where students could come any time, day or night, to gather with their friends and pray for their campus and community. It was an exhilarating time.

Most remarkable during this season was Allison's involvement in a semester of intercession that united some seventy campuses across America in a chain of nonstop student prayer in early 2006. Allison pro-

posed the idea while on a conference call with Campus Renewal Minis-
tries, and the surge of prayer was coordinated by a partnership known
as Campus Transformation Network. In the academic year that followed
(2006–2007), the number of praying campuses increased to 120 through
a timely initiative known as YOPP, the "Year of Partnered Prayer."

In the midst of all the excitement and gathering momentum, how-
ever, there were times of discouragement as well. During one period
in particular, Allison experienced what she later described as an "ex-
treme wilderness" in her journey of faith. God seemed distant. Even
though she kept praying, Allison's faith felt very fragile and increas-
ingly dry, even brittle to the point of breaking.

It was not that Allison had done anything wrong. It was simply that
in all of her activity, she had started to feel as if she was a "tool" for
God instead of a friend of God. Throughout those difficult days, as she
neared the end of her studies, her local church, those humble leaders
who had stood beside her from the very beginning, especially helped
Allison find her way back to the simplicity of prayer and the certainty
of her friendship with God.

In December 2006, Allison graduated from OSU. Even though she
was finished with her studies, it seemed as if there was still something
more for her as it related to campuses and prayer in Ohio. Hearing
stories of what was happening at other colleges and universities
across the state, stories very similar to her own, Allison began dream-
ing and praying about a statewide, collegiate initiative that would
cover "Campus Ohio" in prayer for a full forty days.

And that is why, in late March of 2007, seventy-two students from
eleven campuses gathered in a sacred and beautiful barn, knelt down
beside one another on its smooth hickory floors and started praying
together for Campus Ohio to be transformed by the presence of God.*

---

*Allison Brooks is now the director of Network 50, part of Campus America, an initia-
tive of 24-7 Prayer that is working with students and professors, multiple ministries
and local churches to help create a connected, unbroken year of prayer in 2010 that
involves students from every college and university campus in the United States.
The story of Allison's time at Ohio State was compiled from personal interviews and
correspondence. (See also Love OSU's website <www.loveosu.com> and Campus
Ohio's website <www.campusohio.org>.)

PRAYER IS THE PLACE TO BEGIN

THE CAMPUS OHIO STORY

Campus Ohio. The name is telling in its singularity. . . .

If more university students took hold of the vision, the nation could be transformed one college at a time. Campus Michigan. Campus Indiana. Campus Kansas. Campus Oregon. Campus America. What's beginning in Ohio . . . didn't start because of any national ministry. . . . It was a simple and beautiful seed planted by God in the hearts of a few normal university students.

—RYAN MILNER

The story of Allison Brooks and Campus Ohio is especially compelling because of its simplicity. It is not the story of a perfect strategy or a flawless ministry. Neither is it the story of a fearless and experienced leader who always knew what to do and exactly how to do it. Rather, the story of Allison and what happened in Ohio is the simple story of a student who became fascinated with Jesus by reading the Bible, the story of a student who responded to that fascination by experimenting in prayer, the story of a student who discovered that there were others who wanted to learn how to pray too, the story of a student who realized that there is power in praying *together*.

When the students of Campus Ohio gathered in the Barn Church in early 2007 and began telling their stories to one another, most encouraging of all was the awareness that God was doing something much *bigger* than they imagined. As it turned out, Allison's encouraging account of what was happening at OSU was just one of numerous stories of God leading students to pray throughout Ohio. Lindsay Ellyson, for example, who was studying at Mt. Vernon Nazarene University during that time, had been gathering her friends on campus to pray for an hour every day, five days a week, for five full months. That sort of passion in prayer and consistency in purpose is contagious and holds the potential to "infect" an entire campus with the "epidemic" of awakening.

John Hayward, of the School of Technology at the University of Glamorgan in Wales, has traced the surprising similarities between the contagious nature of viral epidemics and the contagious nature of the spread of the gospel. In both cases the critical factors have to do with the intensity of the "infection" in the first place and the available networks of contagion through which the "virus" can be effectively spread.

To educate the public about the 2009 outbreak of the "Swine Flu," or influenza A (H1N1), the World Health Organization created an interactive online map that tracked the highly contagious virus as it rapidly spread across the planet. The map offers a fascinating glimpse into the viral mechanics that can transform a local virus into a worldwide epidemic. Observing the global effect of the swine flu in action, and especially witnessing the shockingly brief timescale in which it encircled the earth, helps us to understand how one person's health in a small town in Mexico can powerfully influence the health of the whole world.

When we apply that principle to the power of prayer on campus, the point is simply this: *a genuine obsession with Jesus has the potential to be wildly contagious.* The story of Campus Ohio is starting to take place on numerous campuses across the country. It is not a story that is limited to one particular region or a specific demographic. Students at state universities and private colleges, those involved in long-established collegiate ministries and brand new communities of faith, black and white students, Asian and Native American students, Hispanic and visiting international students, each in their own way are beginning to pray.

STORIES OF STUDENT PRAYER ACROSS CAMPUS AMERICA

We pray for the big things, . . . we pray for the small things. It's just a bunch of people hungry for God.

—SLATE STOUT

Arizona State University (ASU) is the second biggest campus in the country, just after Ohio State. More than fifty-one thousand students are enrolled at ASU. In the autumn of 2007, about six months after Campus Ohio, two hundred students at Arizona State determined to cover their campus in prayer for twenty-one days. "All through the day and night," reported an article in *USA Today* that covered the event, "they pray . . . their stillness and quiet in marked contrast to the nearly constant rush of . . . the campus."

Three months after the event at ASU, the *Michigan Daily* covered a similar story at the University of Michigan (UM). Students at UM were involved in a project on campus called "40 Days of Prayer." The report in the *Daily* particularly highlighted the testimony of a sophomore, "who . . . passionately spoke to a captivated crowd about how the 40 Days of Prayer helped her overcome an eating disorder." Multiple groups on campus, including Phi Alpha Kappa, Campus Crusade, World Reach International and New Life Church, sponsored the 2008 event. (One year later, when the event took place again, twenty campus groups were part of the prayer initiative.)

Just one month after the 40 Days of Prayer launched at UM in 2008, the *Columbus Dispatch* reported an incredible story that took place at Ohio University (not to be confused with Ohio State University). "When an . . . employee decided to end his life Friday," the article explains, "students turned to the power of prayer and the pen to save him. It worked."

According to the *Dispatch*, a group of praying students asked God to give them words of encouragement for a suicidal man who was preparing to jump from the ledge of a building on campus. A crisis specialist read the words of encouragement to the distraught man during a four-hour suicide intervention that ultimately saved his life. The following are excerpts from what the *Dispatch* called the "Samaritans' Letters":

> I know sometimes it is easy to feel alone in the world, but it is important to remember that there are people who care. Right now there are a lot of people praying for you. . . . You are not alone, and you are loved.

> I don't know you or what is on your mind. . . . But I do know the pain and brokenness that comes from living in this world. I have suffered from depression for two years, and I know what it feels like to be hopeless at times. But I know there is more. There is beauty. You'll see it if you look.

When people pray on campus, things begin to change. At the sprawling campus of Arizona State this change looked like stillness in the midst of the mad hustle and bustle of fifty-one thousand students. At the University of Michigan it looked like a young woman set free from an eating disorder. At Ohio University it looked like a suicidal employee listening to words of life when he was on the very edge of death. The power of prayer changes things.

At McDaniel College in Maryland this looked like thirteen students deciding to follow Jesus. At Haskell Indian Nations University in Kansas it looked like a young Caucasian woman and an older Native American intercessor weeping together over the sins of history. At Oklahoma State University it looked like a bunch of guys transforming a nineteen-bedroom frat house into a counterculture of Christ-centered community and 24-7 prayer called The Jesus House. The power of prayer changes things.

At Morgan State University, a historically African American institution, this looked like a prayer tent in the center of campus with young black students on their knees in the middle of a late-night storm. At Gardner-Webb University in North Carolina it looked like "a prayer room covered in art and scriptures, a wailing wall with . . . heart cries to the most holy God, a place where students could go spend time with their Creator."

Those that visited the room encountered a wall of prayers and petitions. Real, raw prayers asking God for deliverance from sexual addictions, for suicidal thoughts, healing and release from illness, the salvation of lost friends. They found books full of prayers. . . . They were able to see maps covered with pictures and writing and prayers for different parts of the world. Markers and colored pencils were scattered on the floor from where people had written verses on the wall. From where people had written, "Come, Lord Jesus, Come!"

Whether it is fifty-two days on campuses throughout the state of Georgia or thirty days on campuses across Washington, Oregon, North Dakota and Alaska, students are beginning to realize that the power of prayer changes things.

EXPERIMENTS IN PRAYER: CATALYTIC EVENTS AND NETWORKS OF (HOLY) CONTAGION

When a doctoral student at Princeton asked, "What is
there left in the world for original dissertation research?"
Albert Einstein replied, "Find out about prayer.
Somebody must find out about prayer."

—PHILIP YANCEY

The movement of prayer currently building across the campuses of America is bigger than any one ministry, denomination, local church or organization. At its forefront are very ordinary students marked by an extraordinary passion to "experiment" in prayer. Although there are numerous local, statewide and national ministries partnering together and contributing to the momentum, there is not a centralized structure or single strategy that is essentially directing the movement. Truly it is a grassroots initiative and ordinary, prayerful students are the primary people making it happen.

At the same time, though, there have been (and will surely continue to be) catalytic events and vital networks that serve to inspire and instruct and spread the movement. One of the most well known of these events and networks is the 268 Generation that is behind the Passion conferences. In May of 2000, more than forty thousand students from every state in America gathered on a farm in Tennessee for a Passion event called OneDay, "a solemn assembly of prayer for spiritual awakening in [this] generation." That historic gathering in 2000 was followed by similar events in strategic student hubs like Boston in 2003, where the Passion tour filled the Orpheum Theater with twenty-six hundred students in what proved to be the largest gathering of Christian students in the history of the city.

Representing another part of the burgeoning student prayer movement, and closely connected to the International House of Prayer (IHOP) in Kansas City, are a number of dynamic gatherings, schools and networks associated with TheCall, Onething and the Luke 18 Project. While each of these ministries serve a broader spectrum of people than college and university students alone, they are nonetheless strategically committed to praying for campuses. In particular, the Onething young-adult gatherings and the solemn assemblies of The Call have catalyzed tens of thousands of students into more intentional lifestyles of prayer and fasting.

What is especially encouraging about such catalytic events and critical networks is that many of them are beginning to serve one another in the common cause of prayer. For example, at Urbana 06 (which gathered 23,000 students and missionaries from every state and 140 nations), InterVarsity, Student Volunteer Movement 2 (SVM2) and 24-7 Prayer USA co-created an engaging and informative prayer room called The Journey. Students from the University of Arizona (UA) were so inspired by the experience in prayer that when they returned to their university they pitched a white tent in the center of campus and started a nonstop prayer chain that lasted for forty days. The prayer initiative at AU created such a compelling response that campus police posted a list of requests in the tent, and the *Arizona Daily Wildcat*, the university newspaper, printed a story with the headline: "Students Pray Nonstop."

Because the students from AU were especially inspired by the example of prayerful unity at Urbana, that same sort of unity became a major mark of their prayer movement on campus. "From the beginning," explains Theo Davis, one of the leaders of the initiative at AU, "we fought to keep the vision as simple as we could: unity in the body of Christ." Davis continues:

> We chose to chase after unity in the body, which glorifies God, rather than chasing an agenda. By stripping the event of an agenda, we were free to just create a space where people could go and meet Jesus. This rendered denominational differences irrelevant because almost every Christ-follower values prayer. Some groups would not have participated if we had focused on some of those differences. . . . Our priority was not a picture-perfect prayer event, but simply coming together to glorify God.

THE AGENDA IS JESUS

So this guy comes up to me and says,
"What's the vision? What's the big idea?"
I open my mouth and words come out like this . . .
The vision?
The vision is Jesus.
Obsessively, dangerously, undeniably Jesus.

—PETE GREIG

One of the most compelling and controversial things about Jesus is his choice of friends. His disciples, with their various backgrounds and conflicting worldviews, were an unlikely collection of companions, to say the least. Ranging from Matthew the tax collector on the one hand to Simon the Zealot on the other, the polarizing agendas and diverse political perspectives they represented were simply stunning for their first-century setting. That such individuals would willingly follow Jesus *together* was a miracle on par with someone walking on the Sea of Galilee.*

For the friends and followers of Jesus, it was not as if the controversial issues of their time no longer mattered to them, it was simply that Jesus *mattered more*. Clearly, the disciples still had their differences, but because of Jesus, those differences were no longer the things that defined them. Their unity was not based on abandoning their principles or on compromising the concerns that were closest to their hearts; rather, their unity was based on the fact that Jesus had called the disciples to follow him *together*. In John 17, shortly before Jesus is betrayed and arrested, he prayed for his disciples to become one:

> I am praying not only for these disciples but also for all who will ever believe in me through their message. I pray that they will all be one, just as you and I are one—as you are in me, Father, and I am in you. . . .
>
> May they experience such perfect unity that the world will know that you sent me and that you love them as much as you love me. (John 17:20-23)

The greatest test in the emerging student prayer movement is whether or not we will love and respect, serve and honor one another even when we disagree. Forging such relationships will undoubtedly demand real humility. But if we are willing to learn from one another, as the students at Arizona University did, and to get down on our knees side-by-side in the place of prayer, always remembering that the agenda is ultimately Jesus, we may just discover that we stand up much stronger *together*.

---

*This may explain why the Gospel of Luke records that Jesus spent the entire night in prayer before he called his disciples (Luke 6:12-16). When you take into account the disciples' differing viewpoints and competing perspectives, one cannot help but wonder if Jesus spent the whole night in prayer because he was praying, "Father, are you sure these guys will be able to get along with each other?"

FINDING YOUR PLACE IN HISTORY

When God intends great mercy for His people,
He first sets them praying.

—MATTHEW HENRY

Historically speaking, we are probably in the middle of the most widespread movement of prayer Christianity has ever experienced. Most extraordinary is the fact that so many different groups, from so many different backgrounds, in so many different places are praying *together*. In 2010 an initiative of 24-7 Prayer called Campus America is partnering with students and professors, long-established collegiate ministries and brand new communities of faith to help connect every college and university campus in the United States in a chain of non-stop student prayer for an entire year. With the help of Allison Brooks and many others, it is time to make the historic journey from Campus Ohio to Campus America, and it all begins in the place of prayer.

1. As you "experiment" in prayer, take courage from the words of Charles Spurgeon, a famous nineteenth-century British minister: "Perhaps you think that God will not hear your prayers because you cannot pray grandly like some other person. . . . Be satisfied to offer to God broken language. . . . Go to him with holy familiarity and be not afraid to cry in his presence, *Abba Father*."

2. Let us become the answer to Jesus' unanswered prayer, "Father, make them one . . . that the world will know that you sent me." Are you willing to cooperate with a believer who believes differently than you? Are you willing to put aside nonessentials for the one, true essential: Jesus? Are you willing to pray with someone who does not share your political opinions, remembering that Jesus called the tax collector Matthew and Simon the Zealot to follow him *together?* Unity in prayer does not mean unanimity in opinions, but it does mean that we have to humbly recognize that *none of us have the whole truth*. Are you willing to make your social agendas, as important as they may be, as well as your intellectual pride re-

garding nonessential doctrinal differences, secondary to the centrality of Jesus? "Father, make them one," Jesus said, "that the world will know that you sent me."

3. Whether you are a student, a professor, a parent, a pastor, a ministry leader or simply someone who is willing to pray, visit www.campusamerica.org and see how you can get involved in the 2010 year of nonstop student prayer.

10

Campus America, today. *Alaska Pacific University, Charter College, University of Alaska, Alabama State University, Faulkner University, Heritage Christian University, Athens State University, Judson College, Samford University, Talladega College, United States Sports Academy, University of Alabama, Ecclesia College, John Brown University, Ouachita Baptist University, University of Arkansas, University of the Ozarks, American Indian College of the Assemblies of God, Arizona State University, DeVry University, Grand Canyon University, Northern Arizona University, The Art Institute of Phoenix, University of Arizona, Azusa Pacific University, Biola University, Chapman University, Dongguk Royal University, Fuller Theological Seminary, Occidental College, Pacific Lutheran Theological Seminary, Pepperdine University, Point Loma Nazarene University, Silicon Valley College, Stanford University, The National Hispanic University, University of California, University of Southern California, Westmont College, Colorado Christian University, Colorado School of Mines, Denver Seminary, Fort Lewis College, Rocky Mountain College of Art and Design, United States Air Force Academy, University of Colorado, Westwood College, Bais Binyomin Academy, Connecticut College, Hartford Seminary, Holy Apostles College and Seminary, United States Coast Guard Academy, University of Connecticut, Wesleyan University, Yale University, American University, George Washington University, Georgetown University, Howard University, University of the District of Columbia, Delaware State University, Widener University, Ave Maria University, Clearwater Christian College, Edison College, Florida Gulf Coast University, Florida State University, Full Sail University, Hobe Sound Bible College, Saint Leo University, St. Petersburg College, University of Central Florida, University of Miami, Agnes Scott College, Atlanta College of Art, Columbia Theological Seminary, Emory University, Gainesville State College, Georgia Institute of Technology, Geor-*

gia State University, Kennesaw State University, Mercer University, Savannah State University, The Art Institute of Atlanta, Toccoa Falls College, University of Georgia, Hawaii Pacific University, University of Hawaii, University of the Nations, Coe College, Des Moines University, Drake University, Grinnell College, Hamilton College, Iowa State University, University of Iowa, Waldorf College, Boise State University, Lewis-Clark State College, University of Idaho, DePaul University, Hebrew Theological College, Judson University, Knox College, Loyola University of Chicago, Millikin University, North Park University, Northwestern University, Rush University, University of Chicago, Wheaton College, Anderson University, Ball State University, DePauw University, Huntington University, Indiana Wesleyan University, Purdue University, Taylor University, University of Indianapolis, University of Notre Dame, Valparaiso University, Friends University, Haskell Indian Nations University, Kansas State University, MidAmerica Nazarene University, Newman University, University of Kansas, Wichita State University, Asbury College, Frontier School of Midwifery and Family Nursing, Kentucky State University, Saint Catherine College, The Southern Baptist Theological Seminary, University of the Cumberlands, Louisiana State University, Loyola University, Our Lady of the Lake College, Tulane University of Louisiana, University of New Orleans, Xavier University, Amherst College, Berklee College of Music, Boston University, Brandeis University, Clark University, College of the Holy Cross, Gordon College, Harvard University, Massachusetts Institute of Technology, Mount Holyoke College, Northeastern University, Smith College, Tufts University, University of Massachusetts, Wellesley College, Williams College, Worcester Polytechnic Institute, Baltimore International College, Hood College, Johns Hopkins University, Ner Israel Rabbinical College, Sojourner-Douglass College, United States Naval Academy, Bangor Theological Seminary, Colby College, Maine Maritime Academy, Unity College, University of Maine, Alma College, Andrews University, Baker College, Calvin College, Cornerstone University, Davenport University, Eastern Michigan University, Kalamazoo College, Michigan State University, Sacred Heart Major Seminary, The Robert B. Miller College, University of Michigan, Acad-

emy College, Bethel University, Brown College, Martin Luther College, Minnesota State University, Oak Hills Christian College, St. Olaf College, University of Minnesota, Assemblies of God Theological Seminary, Avila University, College of the Ozarks, Grantham University, Kansas City College, Midwest University, Missouri State University, Saint Louis University, University of Missouri, William Jewell College, Alcorn State University, Belhaven College, Jackson State University, Mississippi University for Women, University of Mississippi, Rocky Mountain College, Salish Kootenai College, The University of Montana, Yellowstone Baptist College, Bennett College for Women, Catawba College, Duke University, Gardner-Webb University, John Wesley College, North Carolina School of the Arts, Peace College, St. Andrews Presbyterian College, University of North Carolina, Wake Forest University, Aakers College, North Dakota State University, Sitting Bull College, Turtle Mountain Community College, Bellevue University, Creighton University, Dana College, Grace University, Midland Lutheran College, The Creative Center, Antioch University, Dartmouth College, Magdalen College, Plymouth State University, Thomas More College of Liberal Arts, University of New Hampshire, Beth Medrash Govoha, New Jersey City University, Princeton Theological Seminary, Princeton University, Rutgers University, The College of New Jersey, College of Santa Fe, Eastern New Mexico University, Institute of American Indian and Alaska Native Culture, New Mexico State University, Sierra Nevada College, University of Nevada, Bais Medrash Elyon, Christ the King Seminary, Colgate University, Columbia University, Cornell University, Culinary Institute of America, Hebrew Union College, Hofstra University, Houghton College, Manhattan School of Music, New York Academy of Art, Saint Vladimirs Orthodox Theological Seminary, Sarah Lawrence College, Stony Brook University, SUNY, Syracuse University, The Juilliard School, The New School, Bryant and Stratton College, Defiance College, Lake Erie College, Malone College, Mount Vernon Nazarene University, Oberlin College, Ohio State University, Ohio Wesleyan University, Xavier University, Bacone College, Langston University, Oklahoma Christian University, Oral Roberts University, University of Oklahoma, Birthingway College of Midwifery,

Gutenberg College, National College of Natural Medicine, Oregon College of Art and Craft, Pacific University, Reed College, Byzantine Catholic Seminary, Carnegie Mellon University, DeSales University, Eastern University, International Institute for Restorative Practices, Messiah College, Moravian College, Pennsylvania State University, Swarthmore College, Temple University, Thomas Jefferson University, Brown University, Rhode Island School of Design, Roger Williams University, College of Charleston, Columbia International University, Converse College, Southern Wesleyan University, University of South Carolina, Oglala Lakota College, Si Tanka University, University of Sioux Falls, University of South Dakota, Belmont University, Cumberland University, Fisk University, King College, Sewanee: The University of the South, The University of Tennessee, Union University, Vanderbilt University, Baylor University, Dallas Theological Seminary, Rice University, Southwestern Assemblies of God University, Texas A & M University, The Art Institute of Dallas, The University of Texas, Wiley College, Brigham Young University, University of Utah, Westminster College, College of William and Mary, Eastern Mennonite University, George Mason University, Hampden-Sydney College, Liberty University, Shenandoah University, University of Richmond, University of Virginia, Washington and Lee University, Burlington College, Green Mountain College, Johnson State College, School for International Training, University of Vermont, Mars Hill Graduate School, Seattle Pacific University, University of Washington, Walla Walla University, Whitworth College, Beloit College, Lawrence University, Milwaukee School of Engineering, Sacred Heart School of Theology, University of Wisconsin, Viterbo University, Appalachian Bible College, Bethany College, Shepherd University, West Virginia Wesleyan College, University of Wyoming.[*]

---

[*]A complete listing of the more than 2,600 four-year colleges, universities, institutes and seminaries in the United States would require twenty-eight pages of print, not including over 1600 junior and community colleges, as well as numerous unaccredited institutions that practice a nontraditional approach to education. This partial listing, representing campuses from all fifty states, is a sampling of Campus America.

WHEN OUR PRAYERS BECOME PRACTICAL

THE ANATOMY OF TRANSFORMATION

Once Jesus was in a certain place praying. As he finished,
one of his disciples came to him and said, "Lord, teach us
to pray."

—LUKE 11:1

Considering the sacred causes and global effects that have helped shape the unfolding history of colleges and universities from the very beginning, we cannot help but wonder what might happen should a movement of student prayer seriously begin to reengage campuses with God today. If the past provides any encouraging clues about the future, then the stories of Henry Dunster at Harvard and the Wesley brothers at Oxford, Grace Wilder at Mount Holyoke and John Mott at Cornell, Bill Borden at Yale and Allison Brooks at Ohio State, together with the many other lives and movements we have considered in this book, should inspire us with great hope. Prayer changes things.

The primary reason we pray, however, is not because of the change that may or may not come as a result of our prayers. Nor do we primarily pray because of the inspiring stories of those who have gone before us. The principal reason we pray is because Jesus taught us to pray. Following Jesus, which is ultimately what Christianity is all about, is a lifelong journey of learning to live as Jesus lived, and that includes learning how to pray even as Jesus prayed. "Are you tired? Worn out? Burned out on religion?" Jesus asked his followers, "Come to me," he continued:

> Get away with me and you'll recover your life. I'll show you how to take a real rest. Walk with me and work with me—watch how I do it. Learn the unforced rhythms of grace. I won't lay anything heavy or ill-fitting on you. Keep company with me and you'll learn to live freely and lightly. (Matthew 11:28-30 *The Message*)

When Jesus called the disciples to follow him, he was essentially inviting them to become like him. He was inviting the disciples to interpret Torah and the biblical narrative in the way that he did, to practice mercy in the way that he did, to heal the sick and cast out demons in the way that he did, to know God in the way that he did. The most important calling of first-century disciples was to become like their rabbi (*rabbi* means "master" or "teacher").

Taking into account that central calling, it is deeply significant that the disciples specifically asked of Jesus, "Lord, teach us to pray." Having closely observed the sacred rhythms and extraordinary seasons of prayer that guided their rabbi's life, it was as if the dearest friends and followers of Jesus recognized prayer as the open secret of his unusual communion with the One he called Father.

Like most devout Jews of his time, Jesus would have prayed the ancient Hebrew creed called the Shema on a daily basis. Composed of words from Deuteronomy 6:4-9 and two other passages of Scripture as well, the Shema was meant to remind the Hebrew people of what it meant practically to love God individually and in community. Undoubtedly the disciples would have prayed this prayer with Jesus during their rhythms of daily worship together. Also, according to the Gospel narratives, Jesus regularly took time for prayer on his own and encouraged his disciples to do the same. Reciting the Shema with his friends and making time to pray in solitude were two of the spiritual disciplines or sacred rhythms that marked the prayer life of Jesus.

Alongside his daily rhythms of prayer, there were extraordinary seasons of prayer in Jesus' life as well. For example, he spent forty days in prayer and fasting before launching his messianic kingdom movement that completely redefined the terms of Torah and what it meant to be Israel (Matthew 4:1-11). Jesus then spent an entire night in prayer before he chose the twelve disciples who would become the revolutionary carriers of his kingdom (Luke 6:12-16). And finally, before he went to the cross to forever remake humanity through his suffering, death and resurrection, Jesus prayed with such astonishing passion that he sweat drops of blood (Luke 22:39-44).

Every extraordinary period of prayer in the life of Jesus preceded a vital and very definite shift in his ministry. These unusual moments of intercession marked the critical turning points of his life and were always in advance of some specific purpose his Father was leading him toward. Lasting anywhere from a few hours to forty days, such extraordinary prayer seemingly prepared Jesus for what was coming next.

If God is indeed calling college and university students to pray in an extraordinary way at present, then it is most likely because God is preparing students for a very specific purpose. The point is not simply to pack our prayer rooms full of people or to count as many conversions as we can. It is, rather, to pray like Jesus prayed: in steady obedience to God, in honest expectation of authentic and lasting transformation, and with a genuine willingness to do whatever God call us to do.

MISSION, MERCY AND MARKETPLACE

Your kingdom come,

your will be done,

on earth as it is in heaven.

—MATTHEW 6:10 NIV

At last count, according to the U.S. Census Bureau, there were more than 20 million college and university students in the United States. That figure includes 17.1 million undergrads and 3.4 million graduate students. Of that total number, more than 600,000 are international students, representing almost every nation on earth. Although specific enrollment figures for colleges and universities worldwide are more difficult to determine, recent estimates suggest there are between 110 and 130 million students actively involved in full- or part-time study on campuses around the world right now, and over 40 million of those students are studying in China and the United States.

It is important for us to understand the vital role that college and university students play in the world. While their numbers only represent a small fraction of the 6.8 billion people on the planet, their potential influence in every area of culture and society is astounding. "Where do the leaders in these realms come from?" asks Professor Charles Malik in *The Two Tasks*, "They all come from the universities."

> What are they fed, intellectually, morally, spiritually, personally, in the fifteen or twenty years they spend in the school and university, is the decisive question. It is there that the foundations of character and mind and outlook and conviction and attitude and spirit are laid, and to paraphrase a Biblical saying, if the wrong foundations are laid, or if the right foundations are vitiated or undermined, "what can the righteous do?" (Psalm 11:3).

A nonstop year of prayer that connects every campus in America— or *every campus in the world*, for that matter—must not be viewed as the end goal or "holy grail" of our engagement with God. It should be viewed instead as the next step forward in a long and inspiring lineage of faith and education, a holy heritage that has in many ways been abandoned on campus and that is now being humbly reclaimed in the sacred space of prayer. What begins in that sacred space, however, must not end there: this extraordinary season of student prayer must ultimately result in a more Jesus-like engagement with the needs of the world through mission, mercy and marketplace.

* *Mission* is telling the story of Jesus, who he is and what he has done.

* *Mercy* is loving people like Jesus did, and that especially involves loving the poor.

* *Marketplace* is where we live like Jesus, including every area of culture and society.

The kingdom that Jesus talked about is a holistic God-centered reality that utterly remakes our lives. In 2 Corinthians 5:17, the apostle Paul refers to this miraculous transformation as a "new creation" (NIV). Christianity is not simply a religion in fierce competition with other religions, worldviews or any other sort of "ism" (e.g., Christianity vs. Humanism or Christianity vs. Islam, etc.). According to the New Testament, Jesus did not pioneer a new religion at all, and there is in fact no record that he ever even spoke of such a thing. On the contrary—through his life, death and resurrection—the God-man actually pioneered *a new way of being human altogether:* a renewed humanity that celebrates the coming kingdom of God by sharing the gospel, serving the poor, setting slaves free, caring for our planet and loving one another.

Considering the comprehensive and far-reaching embrace of this kingdom, what better place for it to be explored than on a campus, where students are involved in multiple disciplines of study that influence every area of life? Communications and the arts, business and science and technology, education and healthcare and international development, linguistics and diplomacy and intercultural studies, philosophy and history and the humanities: the campus, like few places in the world, is truly a microcosm of the various and vital activities that help to determine the grand direction of humanity. If God is not welcomed on campus, how will God be welcomed in the world?

THE ANATOMY OF TRANSFORMATION: HEART, SOUL, MIND AND STRENGTH

One of the teachers of religious law . . . asked, "Of all the commandments, which is the most important?" Jesus replied, "The most important commandment is this: 'Listen, O Israel! The LORD our God is the one and only LORD. And you must love the LORD your God with all your heart, all your soul, all your mind, and all your strength.'"

—MARK 12:28-30

According to the Scriptures, to love God fully means to love God with every area of our lives, and according to Jesus, such all-consuming love is the most important commandment of all. In translating the passage above for *The Message*, Eugene Peterson rendered the words *heart, soul, mind* and *strength* as "passion and prayer and intelligence and energy." Peterson's point was to help us see those significant words—heart, soul, mind and strength—in all of their original and transformative meaning.

- *Heart* **is what shapes our passion.**
- *Soul* **is what shapes our will.**
- *Mind* **is what shapes our understanding.**
- *Strength* **is what shapes our service.**

When we embrace the *full* anatomy of transformation, rather than just a part, we soon realize that God is as concerned with the secret place of passionate prayer as he is with the marketplace of global ideas. In the mind of the Creator there is no divide between the sacred and the secular. God made it all. Because of this, learning to love God with the entirety of our being, means learning to love God with all of our passion, with all of our prayers, with all of our intelligence and with all of our energy. When we remove any one aspect of love (heart, soul, mind or strength), or when we exclusively focus on one area of love over and above another, we miss the mark of loving God fully.

Passion draws most of us to God in the first place. In fact, even in the formation of a baby in the womb, the *heart* takes shape before the brain. What would life be without laughter, tears, passion or pain? Our emotional connection to God is foundational. At the same time, however, if we only love God with our heart, we may soon discover that our following of Jesus is based on feelings alone, and as anyone who has ever been in a lasting relationship can tell you, a relationship that endures requires a commitment to love when you feel like it *and* when you don't.

Loving God with our *soul* involves our will; it is the portion of our being that chooses to love God, regardless of our emotional ups and downs. Such love includes not only extraordinary periods of prayer but also (and most especially) spiritual disciplines of prayer. It is through the sacred rhythms of simplicity and solitude, confession and celebration, daily devotion and a lifestyle of fasting, that the Holy Spirit enables us to mature in our faith in such a way as to not be ruled by feelings alone.

To avoid the tendency toward drudgery and legalism in such practices, the discipline of loving God with our choices must be rooted in the deep understanding that loving God is not only the right thing to do but is truly the best thing to do. That sort of insight is nurtured by loving God with our *mind*, when we begin to thoughtfully explore and carefully discover reflections of the character and nature of God in the sweeping contours of history and the startling patterns of zoology, in the intricate and essential dance between economic principles and the practice of justice, in the mind-blowing marvels of astronomy and the artistic epiphanies that inspire creative design. Loving God with our mind means the prayer room is no more holy than the classroom.

As is the case with every other aspect of love, though, to exclusively love God with our mind is to fail to love God fully. The result of such exclusivity in this particular area of our lives is that we either become arrogant about all that we think we know (which produces that false sense of intelligence known as cynicism) or in our passionate pursuit to intellectually understand all things, the simplicity of our faith is crushed by the profound mysteries of the mind of God. Sometimes it is deeply comforting to rest in the simple knowledge that God is God and we are not.[*]

When we love God with our heart, soul and mind, it is natural to love God with our *strength* as well: that is, in the daily areas of service to which we are all called. One of the most disempowering and short-sighted misunderstandings in the history of Christianity is that the calling of a pastor or preacher is somehow more sacred than the calling of a research scientist or elementary school teacher. Jesus was no less holy as a carpenter than as a rabbi, was he? Loving God with

---

[*]"True intellectuals," writes Billy Graham in his foreword to Malik's *The Two Tasks*, "are humble people because they know how hard it is to learn."

one's strength means loving God with whatever area of service we have been entrusted, whether that is in a sanctuary or a laboratory, in a carpenter's workshop or a college classroom.

The anatomy of transformation merges the great divide between the secret place and the marketplace, enabling us to love God with all of our passion, with all of our prayers, with all of our intelligence and with all of our energy. That is what loving God looks like in practice: when our heart, soul, mind and strength worship the Creator as one. But according to the teaching of Jesus, loving God does not stop there.

LIKE YOU LOVE YOURSELF

The second [commandment] is equally important:
"Love your neighbor as yourself."

—MARK 12:31

When Jesus was asked what the greatest commandment was, the first part of his response made perfect sense and was most likely expected. While there were numerous laws that governed ancient Hebrew society, all of those laws were premised on the ultimate commandment of loving God, according to Deuteronomy 6:4-9, with all your heart, soul and strength. This holistic view of love was deeply embedded in the psyche of the Hebrew people because it was part of the Shema they prayed aloud together everyday. "Listen, O Israel!" they would say, "The LORD is our God, the LORD alone. And you must love the LORD your God with all your heart, all your soul, and all your strength" (v. 5).

The Shema was the foundational statement of belief that defined Israel's understanding of their unique relationship with God. According to Jesus, however, there was more to that relationship than the Hebrew people understood, and that is why he added a critical component to the ancient and sacred creed. Having acknowledged the foremost commandment of loving God, Jesus then quoted a passage from Leviticus, "The second [commandment]," he said, "is equally important: 'Love your neighbor as yourself.' No other commandment is greater than these."*

The revolutionary nature of this simple amendment to the Shema is that it forever blurs the line between our worship meetings and our justice meetings, between our sacred gatherings for prayer and our practical service to the poor. It means that reconciliation is not simply a distant theological concept that only has to do with saving our souls, but it is also a necessary means of present grace that enables us to love our neighbors even if they are different than us, and to love our enemies even if they are "terrorists."

When Jesus spoke of loving God and loving others as "equally important" commandments, he bridged the unholy divide that so often separates our devotion from our compassion. While there are many ways to love our neighbors, one way of love that must mark every follower of Jesus is a sacrificial commitment to the poor and disadvantaged, those described by Jesus in the Gospel of Matthew as *the least of these:* those who are hungry and thirsty, those who are strangers in a foreign place, those who are cold and have no clothing, and those who are sick and imprisoned (Matthew 25:31-46).

Serving the poor and disadvantaged is something every one of us can do. It demands no degree, but it does require willingness. It offers little acclaim and it means certain sacrifice. The reward is not received in this life but in the life to come. And most startling of all, according to the Gospel, by serving those who are suffering we are actually serving Jesus: "I tell you the truth," he said, "when you did it to one of the least of these, my brothers and sisters, you were doing it to me!" (Matthew 25:40).

Some time ago, a dear friend was studying for a degree in theology. Her faith was severely tested along the way, and as a result God seemed increasingly distant. As we talked and prayed together about her journey, the remedy that seemed best surprised me. It was not reading a book, paying more attention to her devotional life or listening to another lecture about the mysteries of theology. Rather, the

---

*"Instead of a Love-God *Shema*," Scot McKnight explains in *The Jesus Creed*, "it is a Love-God-and-Others *Shema*" (Brewster, Mass.: Paraclete, 2004).

simple remedy was to begin serving the least of these. Truly, God was much nearer than she thought.

FINDING YOUR PLACE IN HISTORY

I pray that from [God's] glorious, unlimited resources he will empower you with inner strength through his Spirit. Then Christ will make his home in your hearts as you trust in him. Your roots will grow down into God's love and keep you strong. And may you have the power to understand, as all God's people should, how wide, how long, how high, and how deep his love is. May you experience the love of Christ, though it is too great to understand fully. Then you will be made complete with all the fullness of life and power that comes from God.

Now all glory to God, who is able, through his mighty power at work within us, to accomplish infinitely more than we might ask or think.

—EPHESIANS 3:16-20

The reason we know about the stories of the students described throughout this book is because their prayers became practical. They not only dreamed of great things with their friends, they went out and did them with all their heart, soul, mind and strength. That is what happens when extraordinary periods of prayer are combined with sacred rhythms of devotion and compassion. The extraordinary times, lasting from a few hours to forty days, enable us to more deeply experience and more thoroughly embrace our purpose in life. The ongoing rhythms of prayer, day in and day out, remind us that every moment is sacred to God, not just the time spent in the prayer room.

1. Practically examine your devotion to God: heart, soul, mind and strength.

2. Prayerfully consider your compassion toward others, especially the least of these.

3. Always remember the reason we love is because God first loved us.

The secret to finding your place in history is by embracing your identity in God's story. It is a story that began long before colleges and universities were ever even in the mind of humanity, and it is a story that will continue long after campuses—at least as we know them—have ceased to exist. That story, older than time itself, did not start with you or me, nor is it ultimately dependent on you or me. The story of God began with God, and surely it could have stopped there— with God alone—but the story of God continued.

For the friends and followers of Jesus, one of the most intriguing aspects of his prayer life was the fact that he regularly called God *Abba*, which is an intimate Aramaic word that means *Father* or *Daddy*, dependent on your stage of life. It was not unknown in Jewish literature for God to be known as *Abba*, but apparently the way Jesus used the word was startling in its familiarity. While it is clear from the Gospels that Jesus called God *Abba* in reference to the unique and special relationship they shared (which is one of the reasons his ministry was so very controversial), it is equally clear that Jesus invited his followers to also use the word *Abba* or *Father* when talking to God.

Finding your place in history does not begin by boldly attempting to make your mark on history. It begins by knowing you are accepted as God's child. The wonder of God's love is that we do not have to make a place for ourselves in the story of God. Rather, because of Jesus, a place in his story has already been made for us. And that is why we can pray, even as Jesus taught us to pray:

Our Father in heaven,
may your name be kept holy.
May your Kingdom come soon.
May your will be done on earth,
    as it is in heaven.
Give us today the food we need,

and forgive us our debts,
> as we have forgiven our debtors.

And don't let us yield to temptation,
> but rescue us from the evil one.

For yours is the kingdom and the power and the glory forever. Amen.*

---

*This version of the Lord's Prayer is from the New Living Translation. "Forgive us our debts, / as we have forgiven our debtors" is imported from the New International Version, as it is more in keeping with the original Greek. "For yours is the kingdom and the power and the glory forever. Amen" is a line found in later manuscript copies of the Gospel of Matthew; it's included in contemporary translations as a text note.

AFTERWORD

THE "DECISIVE MOMENT" OF OUR LIVES

.

If every Christian student in America prepared themselves for collegiate life by reading *God on Campus* prayerfully, alongside their Bible, I have little doubt that the impact would eventually be felt in every sphere of society and to the ends of the earth.

It's not just that *God on Campus* is challenging for those of us whose hearts have grown weary or hard. Neither is it just that the book is unquenchably optimistic in a cynical age. Trent Sheppard isn't writing merely to help Christian students understand the relevance of their spiritual heritage. At a time when there are 74 percent fewer Christians on U.S. campuses than in the population at large, Trent has his sights clearly set on the ultimate question of God's purposes for our generation. In answering this question he dares to give the campuses their story back—brazenly defying those institutions that have become embarrassed by their own spiritual DNA and have thus become confused about their identity and vocation.

The fact is that whenever a significant minority of students have truly given themselves to live at the intersection of prayer, mission and justice, lives have been changed. One hundred years ago, one of the most extraordinary instances of such an uprising culminated in a historic gathering in Edinburgh, Scotland, which truly touched the ends of the earth. In June 1910, the "World Missionary Conference"

drew 1355 delegates from 160 missions agencies to conspire auda-
ciously for "the evangelization of the world in this generation." Some
historians have described it as the defining moment in the modern
missions and ecumenical movements.

The conference was presided over by John Mott, a familiar figure
in this book as the founding leader of the Student Volunteer Movement, which mobilized 20,000 students onto the global mission field,
shot out like rockets from the places of prayer that were multiplying
on America's campuses at that time. For Mott it had all begun when he
himself was an ambitious young man at Cornell University, whose
faith was peripheral to his drive for worldly success. One cold night in
January 1886, John Mott happened to arrive late at a campus meeting, just in time to hear the British evangelist J. K. Studd issue an appeal: "Seekest thou great things for thyself?" boomed the preacher.
"Seek them not. Seek ye first the Kingdom of God."

This simple challenge shook Mott to the core of his being. Suddenly he realized that the ambition stirring his soul was mere selfishness. Unable to sleep that night, he sought out the Englishman for a
private conversation. "It was," he recalled, "the decisive hour of my
life."

DECADE OF GLOBAL REVIVAL

Twenty-four years later Mott—along with all the delegates gathered in
Scotland—sensed that the fulfillment of Christ's great commission in
their generation was possible. Look at the evidence:

- **For six years revival had been shaking Wales under the leadership
  of a young man called Evan Roberts. Thousands had turned to
  Christ since its inception in 1904, and society was being transformed by the gospel.**

- **In the United States and United Kingdom, the teaching of great
  evangelists such as Dwight L. Moody and Hudson Taylor had captured the hearts and minds of a rising generation. As a result, for
  the almost two decades since Mott himself had been at Cornell,
  successive generations of students had been praying and giving
  themselves sacrificially to mission.**

- And then, in 1906—just four years before the Edinburgh conference—an outpouring of the Holy Spirit at a multiracial 24-7 prayer meeting in Los Angeles had detonated the worldwide Pentecostal and charismatic renewals.

- Meanwhile, a spiritual awakening in Norway was generally acknowledged to be the greatest revival in that land since the Vikings were first evangelized.

- In India the Christian population had grown by 70 percent in a single year: 1905–1906.

- In the decade preceding the Edinburgh conference, the church in Japan had doubled in size; in Indonesia it had tripled.

The rumbling thunder of so many lightning strikes in so many nations in so short a time must still have been reverberating in the souls of the delegates who converged in Scotland that summer to plot the fulfillment of the Great Commission. Indeed eight bold "Commissions" were addressed by the conference, dealing with such explicit challenges as "Carrying the Gospel to All the Non-Christian World" (on the first day) and "The Promotion of Christian Unity" (on the last day), via discussions about the role of national governments and "Education in Relation to the Christianization of National Life." These were big but important conversations for people with such a vast vision.

WHAT'S THE BIG IDEA?

It is unfortunate that some people with a global vision have a parochial theology—merely wanting to populate the earth with their own brand. Others have a big theology, but their vision is so limited that they just study, discuss, blog and critique while the poor remain poor and the church continues to decline. One of the inspiring things about *God on Campus* is that it traces the stories of people and movements whose theology made their vision meaningful.

I once asked Trent Sheppard's opinion about a bold, well-intentioned evangelistic initiative aiming to "save many souls."

"What are they going to do with all the bodies?" was his dry reply.

Behind the humor lay an important idea, reflected throughout this book. We're not in the business of saving disembodied souls from sinful flesh, godless campuses and a corrupted world. In line with the Abrahamic covenant, our destiny is to be a blessing, not a curse, to all nations (Genesis 26:2-4). As the apostle Paul explains in 2 Corinthians 5, our commission is to participate in the re-creating of people, the redeeming of cultures, the renewing of creation and the reconciling of all things in Christ. This means that people are as likely to be sent from the place of prayer on campus to Silicon Valley, Skid Alley, Hollywood or Wall Street, as to some remote tribe in a distant land. Evangelization and social transformation walk hand in hand. This is why it is vital that the campuses become, once again, greenhouses for the formation of the spirit and the mind.

Lebanese ambassador Charles Malik, cited several times in this book, was one of the authors of the United Nations Declaration of Human Rights. Speaking at the dedication of the Billy Graham Center at Wheaton College, he argued passionately for the university's role in marrying intellectual and spiritual formation: "At the heart and the mind of the crisis in Western civilization," he said, "lies the state of mind and the spirit in the universities. Christ being the Light of the World, His light must be brought to bear on the problem of the formation of the mind. . . . Therefore how can evangelism consider its task accomplished if it leaves the university unevangelized? This," he concluded, "is the great task, the historic task, the most needed task required loud and clear by the Holy Ghost himself."

"SPIRITUAL" WARFARE

Such big vision is easily criticized, of course. The World Missionary Conference was certainly disparaged by subsequent generations for the sheer audacity of its goals. Some have even accused Mott and his friends of arrogance in believing that they could fulfill the great commission. But whatever we make of their buccaneering spirit, the apostolic passion firing their hearts is surely beyond contention. Each had known their own "decisive moment" of commitment to the gospel of Christ. And as another zealot once wrote, in a letter to the adherents of a novel Jewish sect who were living as a despised minority in the heart of the Roman super-power: *"I am not ashamed of the gospel, because it is the power of God for the salvation of everyone who believes"* (Romans 1:16).

At the forefront of the Edinburgh conference were representatives from three great mission-sending nations of the time, all of which had been stirred by the recent movements of prayer: the United States, the United Kingdom and Germany. It is therefore chilling to pause and recognize that within four years of the World Missionary Conference, the brightest and best of these three great nations, poised to fulfill the great commission, would instead begin destroying one another in two world wars. Tens of thousands of those saved in campus meetings and Welsh valleys bled and died in the French trenches. It is sobering to realize how violent the backlash when Satan is confronted with the possibility of Christ's return (Matthew 24:14). Perhaps we should therefore just lay down our banners a while and simply count the cost of our prayers for revival and social transformation.

However, the legacy of that Edinburgh conference lives on in the modern missions movement, in the World Council of Churches (which it was instrumental in forming), in the enduring witness of men like John Mott (who went on to be awarded the Nobel Peace Prize at the end of the Second World War for his missions work) and ultimately in the inspiring story of a generation of students rising up to bless the nations because they first learned to bow the knee in surrendered prayer.

DIVINE SYMMETRY

In the coming years, we're convinced, many students will—like John Mott at Cornell—encounter "the decisive moment" of their lives as the campuses reverberate once again with the call to prayer. We never planned it this way, but it has been pointed out that the Campus America initiative—just one aspect of the Lord's work on campuses—happens to kick off in the centenary year of the World Missionary Conference. This was itself incubated by a previous movement of prayer on the campuses of America. Whether this has occurred by coincidence or divine symmetry, the story of that great gathering a century ago—

and the many extraordinary stories recounted in this book—should shoot adrenaline into our veins, terrifying and inspiring us to pray.

Trent Sheppard leaves us in no doubt that God is on campus. In the words of his dream, storm clouds are gathering. And while the kings of this age eat and drink, we hear the sound of a heavy rain. And so, of course, we pray . . .

> Elijah said to Ahab, "Go, eat and drink, for there is the sound of a heavy rain." . . . But Elijah climbed to the top of Carmel, bent down to the ground and put his face between his knees. (1 Kings 18:41-42)

Pete Greig
24-7 Prayer/Alpha International
Guildford, England
Autumn 2009

ACKNOWLEDGMENTS

Writing a book can be a very vulnerable journey, particularly when the content is close to your heart. The journey of *God on Campus* repeatedly laid my soul bare, and there were two people in whom I especially found refuge and wisdom, prayer and inspiration.

My wife (who was pregnant with our first child and completing her master's degree during the writing) and my mother (an English teacher and former journalist) read every word of the manuscript and believed in the book's message even when I began to doubt.

Bronwyn, this book is yours as much as it is mine. You're my best friend and I love you.

Dear Mom, I reckon King Lemuel said it best: "Her children arise and call her blessed . . ."

Also, many thanks to:

Our family in Greenwood (Dad and Mom), Izmir (Mom Bonnie), Port Stewart (Tré and Tori, Aidan and Elena), Lee's Summit (Mark and Krista, Arianna, Hudson and Hunter), Mesa (BR) and Wheaton (Joellah)—to be loved by all of you is the best of all.

Our *koinonia* at 94 Woodland Street (2007–2009)—thank you, brothahs and sistahs, for the enduring prayers, honest polylogue and pear-tree dining. (And especially to Luke: "Congratulations, it's a book!" will not be soon forgotten, Chief.)

Pete—for calling and telling me what God told you in early 2005, for welcoming Bronwyn and me into the journey called Campus America, and for inviting/charging me to write this book.

The small collection of friends and family who help us do what we do—without each of you I could not have made the space to research and write in the first place. Thank you, thank you, thank you. (Daniel and Lavanchy, I lean on you.)

Black, Wendy and Rusty, and the rest of the CA team—this thing is just getting started, eh? (Ms. All-is-on, I'm particularly grateful to you for letting me tell your story.)

Josh and Rebecca, and the STATUS and LoveWorks crew—you became family to us during 2007–2009, and we miss you, friends.

My landlord and friend, Leon—for the courthouse desk and antique globe, the classic stories and third-floor home—but especially for the friendship. And also to Matt, my downstairs neighbor in Worcester—you helped keep me sane and laughing, you legend.

The libraries at College of the Holy Cross, Clark University and Gordon-Conwell Theological Seminary were especially useful for research, and my friend and editor at IVP, Dave Z., was a model of patience and encouragement along the way.

And finally, to the tribe called YWAM, my family in ministry for years, particularly that eclectic posse of people known as The Factory—Dear Friends, the prayers we prayed were not in vain. Aslan is on the move.

Soli Deo Gloria.

AUTHOR'S NOTE

When I was a little boy, I knew an elderly Irishman with the most wonderful accent I had ever heard. "Hi, Chum," he used to always ask me, "how's your thumb?"

J. Edwin Orr (1912–1987) was the leading revival and spiritual awakening historian of the twentieth century. In the winter years of his life, he mentored my parents, and it was then that I knew him.

Orr was in his seventies during that time, with wispy white hair and eyes so full of wisdom that they seemed to brim with understanding. He had four earned doctorate degrees, but he still treated my brother and sister and me as if there was something quite special he might yet learn from us. Dr. Orr was exceptionally rare in that way.

In 1971, Orr wrote *Campus Aflame: Dynamic of Student Religious Revolution,* a scholarly history of spiritual awakenings in collegiate communities. I mention it here because this book was the most significant source of material in helping me track down the histories that are behind the stories in *God on Campus.*

Dr. Orr died before I was old enough to talk with him about campus awakenings and student movements, but his legacy undoubtedly lives on through the many people he impacted, the numerous books he wrote and the unyielding prayers he prayed. I will always be grateful that I knew him.

ABOUT CAMPUS AMERICA

Campus America is a simple call for a connected, unbroken year of prayer in 2010 to link every college and university campus in the United States in a chain of nonstop student prayer.

The goal is not a new organization. The goal is people praying on campuses.

That's why Campus America is partnering with students and professors, long-established collegiate ministries and brand new communities of faith to make this happen. We are well aware there are numerous campus ministries with more experience and better strategies than we have, and we're calling every one of them to pray.

Why? Because we're convinced if we get down on our knees side-by-side, we'll stand up much stronger together. Unified and humble prayer around the person of Jesus is a powerful prescription for the ills of our time.

Campus America is an initiative of 24-7 Prayer and is all about helping to create sacred space for students to encounter Jesus and to practically engage with the defining issues of this generation.

For more information on Campus America and 24-7 Prayer, visit the following sites:

campusamerica.org
24-7prayer.com

NOTES

Introduction

p. 9   "Who, then, can help the religious soul in the great universities": Charles Habib Malik, *A Christian Critique of the University* (Downers Grove, Ill.: InterVarsity Press, 1982), p. 98.

p. 9   "I put up my thumb": Neil Armstrong, quoted in "Neil Armstrong," International Space Hall of Fame at the New Mexico Museum of Space History, accessed July 20, 2009, at <www.nmspacemuseum.org/halloffame/detail.php?id=1>.

p. 10   "All [people] dream: but not equally": T. E. Lawrence, *Seven Pillars of Wisdom: A Triumph* (New York: Anchor Books, 1991), p. 24.

p. 12   "We had better": N.T. Wright, *The Challenge of Jesus* (Downers Grove, Ill.: InterVarsity Press, 1999), pp. 148-49.

p. 14   "They believed that God was going to do": N. T. Wright, *Surprised by Hope* (New York: Macmillan, 1954), p. 160.

p. 14   "Then instantly the pale brightness": C. S. Lewis, *The Horse and His Boy* (New York: HarperCollins, 1994).

p. 15   college-age young people called The Factory: The Factory was part of Youth With A Mission, an international Christian organization committed to telling people about Jesus, taking care of the poor and needy, and spreading the goodness of God through practical training and education (www.ywam.org).

p. 19   "Truth is not abstract ideas or mystical experiences": Lesslie Newbigin, quoted by Tim Stafford, "God's Missionary to Us," *Christianity Today*, December 9, 1996.

p. 19   "This great, overwhelming movement": Thomas Cahill, *The Gifts of the Jews* (New York: Doubleday, 1998), p. 239.

Chapter 1: Harvard's First Heretic

p. 28   "I am not the man you take me to be": Henry Dunster, *Considerations* (1654) in Jeremiah Chaplin, *Life of Henry Dunster* (Boston: James R. Osgood and Company, 1872), p. 156.

p. 28   accusations that his wife: Samuel Morison, *Three Centuries of Harvard* (Cambridge, Mass: Harvard University Press, 1942), p. 10.

p. 30   Martin Luther, the "solitary professor": R. Tudor Jones, *The Great*

Reformation (Bridgend, U.K.: Bryntirion, 1997), p. 44.

p. 31   "the humiliating journey of openness": A remarkable example of such openness is the Reconciliation Walk. For more information, see Tomas Dixon, "Jerusalem: Reconciliation Walk Reaches Pinnacle," *ChristianityToday*, September 6, 1999 <www.ctlibrary.com/ct/1999/september6/9ta024.html>.

p. 31   They were determined to found a new Cambridge": Samuel Morison, *The Founding of Harvard College* (Cambridge, Mass.: Harvard University Press, 1935), p. 5.

p. 31   Cartwright gave a series of controversial lectures: A. F. Scott Pearson, *Thomas Cartwright and Elizabethan Puritanism 1535–1603* (Gloucester, Mass.: Peter Smith, 1966), pp. 33-43.

p. 32   "I hear that you have erected a Puritan foundation": Sargent Bush Jr. and Carl J. Rasmussen, *The Library of Emmanuel College, Cambridge, 1584–1637* (Cambridge: Cambridge University Press, 1986), p. 2.

p. 32   "Truth is not only that which awaits discovery": Robert Fong, "Called to Teach," *Finding God at Harvard*, ed. Kelly M. Kullberg (Downers Grove, Ill.: InterVarsity Press, 2007), p. 305.

p. 32   "Samuel presided over the world's first university": Morison, *Founding of Harvard College,* p. 5.

p. 33   "Let every student be plainly instructed": *New Englands First Fruits* (1643). (For further information, see James D. Hart and Phillip W. Leininger, "New Englands First Fruits," *The Oxford Companion to American Literature* [Oxford: Oxford University Press, 1995], accessed October 8, 2009, at <1O123-NewEnglands FirstFruits.html>).

p. 33   "desiring to be as gods, we become as devils": Henry Dunster, quoted in Morison, *Founding of Harvard*, p. 251.

p. 34   "Knowledge and virtue are not identical": Jaroslav Pelikan, *The Idea of the University: A Reexamination* (New Haven, Conn.: Yale University Press, 1992), p. 21.

p. 34   Harvard, William & Mary, Yale and Princeton: For a scholarly exploration of America's earliest colleges, see J. David Hoeveler, *Creating the American Mind: Intellect and Politics in the Colonial Colleges* (New York: Rowman & Littlefield, 2002).

p. 34   "The Christian college has no need to apologize": J. Edwin Orr, *Campus Aflame: A History of Evangelical Awakenings in Collegiate Communities* (Wheaton, Ill.: International Awakening Press, 1994), p. 15.

Chapter 2: How Students Shape History

p. 41   "It may be observed, the first rise of Methodism": John Wesley, *A Short History of the People Called Methodist* (1781), quoted in *The Works of John Wesley*, ed. Rupert E. Davies (Nashville: Abingdon, 1989), 9:430.

pp. 41-42   "dramatically altered the course of Western, and in time, global history": For more on "Methodism's rise from a small coterie of religious societies in Oxford University in the 1730s to a major world communion by the beginning of the twentieth century," see especially David Hempton, *Methodism: Empire of the Spirit* (New Haven: Yale University Press, 2005), p. 202 and passim.

p. 42   "He had neither the presumption": John Gambold's letter was written to the Wesley family during John and Charles's failed missionary venture in Georgia, 1735–1738, and is quoted in Whitehead, *Life of Wesley*, p. 284.

p. 43   "Their undertaking included these several particulars": Ibid.

p. 44   "they were out of tune with contemporary cynicism": Gill, *Charles Wesley the First Methodist*, p. 41.

p. 44   506 of 2,000 houses were gin shops: David Lyle Jeffrey, ed., *English Spirituality in the Age of Wesley* (Grand Rapids: Eerdmans, (1987), p. 9.

p. 44   "I went to America, to convert the Indians": John Wesley, *Journal of John Wesley* (Chicago: Moody Press, 1951), p. 53.

p. 45   "I hardly ever knew him go through a sermon without weeping": Cornelius Winter, quoted in Stout, *Divine Dramatist*, p. 41.

p. 46   Massachusetts minister Jonathan Edwards: Robert W. Caldwell III and Douglas A. Sweeny, "Edwards, Jonathan," in *Biographical Dictionary of Evangelicals*, ed. Timothy Larsen (Downers Grove, Ill.: InterVarsity Press, 2003), p. 201.

p. 46   Edwards worked to articulate the "saving affections and experiences": Edwards's classic work on the subject, originally published in 1746, is *The Religious Affections* (Carlisle, Penn.: Banner of Truth Trust, 1961), p. 19.

p. 47   New Lights and Old Lights: For a great discussion on the New Light–Old Light divide during the Great Awakening and its impact on colonial colleges, see George M. Marsden, *The Soul of the American University* (New York: Oxford University Press, 1994), pp. 52-59.

p. 47   "The Gospel of Christ knows no religion but social": John Wesley, quoted in S. Paul Schilling, *Methodism and Society in Theological Perspective* (New York: Abingdon, 1960), p. 61.

p. 48   "Christianity is essentially a social religion": John Wesley, quoted in *John and Charles Wesley: Selected Prayers, Hymns, Journal Notes, Sermons, Letters and Treatises*, ed. Frank Whaling (New York: Paulist Press, 1981), p. 58.

p. 48   "whole series of sporadic and often geographically localized": Howard Snyder, *The Radical Wesley* (Downers Grove, Ill.: InterVarsity Press, 1980), p. 57.

p. 48   "There were obvious weaknesses at work": See E. P. Thompson, *The Making of the English Working Class* (New York: Pantheon Books, 1964), p. 358; and Eric Williams, *Capitalism and Slavery* (New York: Russell & Russell, 1961), p. 181.

p. 49   It was not the economists who liberated the slaves": Kenneth E. Boulding, quoted in Schilling, *Methodism and Society*, p. 64.

Chapter 3: Riots and Revival at Princeton

p. 55   "Have you heard the terrible news from Princeton?" Letter from Rev. Samuel Miller of the New York Presbyterian Church to Rev. E. D. Griffin regarding the riots of 1807, Quoted in Wertenbaker, *Princeton: 1746-1896*, p. 145.

p. 55   typical student at Harvard in the early 1790s: Samuel Morison, *Three Centuries of Harvard* (Cambridge, Mass.: Harvard University Press, 1942), p. 185.

p. 56   complication of campus divide between college and seminary: Mark Noll, *The Scandal of the Evangelical Mind* (Grand Rapids: Eerdmans, 1994), pp. 18-21.

p. 56   "Christianity . . . is not the same as American culture": George M. Marsden and Bradley J. Longfield, eds., *The Secularization of the Academy* (New York: Oxford University Press, 1992), p. 31.

p. 57   "The revivals of the 1730s and 1740s": Mark Noll, *America's God*, quoted in Gary Wills, *Head and Heart: American Christianities* (New York: Penguin, 2007), p. 101.

p. 57   34 towns, 9 communities and 25 settlements: Allen Guelzo "The Great Awakening (1739–1745)," *Encyclopedia of Religious Revivals in America*, ed. Michael McClymond (Westport, Conn.: Greenwood Press, 2001), pp. 193-94.

p. 57   "No books are in request but those of piety": Benjamin Franklin, quoted in Wills, *Head and Heart*, p. 103.

p. 59   "The majority of revivalists undoubtedly preferred": David S. Lovejoy, *Religious Enthusiasm in the New World* (Cambridge, Mass.: Harvard University Press, 1985), p. 184.

p. 60   1750 to 1790 marked by serious decline in active faith: See especially Mark Noll, *America's God: From Jonathan Edwards to Abraham Lincoln* (New York: Oxford University Press, 2002), and the "Rates of Religious Adherence, 1776–2000" in Wills, *Head and Heart*, p. 8.

p. 60   "Between the Christianity of this land": Frederick Douglass, *Narrative of the Life of Frederick Douglass, an American Slave* (1845), quoted in Gregory Boyd, *The Myth of a Christian Nation* (Grand Rapids: Zondervan, 2005), p. 101.

p. 61   "The problem is not only to win souls": Charles Malik, "The Two Tasks," *The Two Tasks of the Christian Scholar: Redeeming the Soul, Redeeming the Mind*, ed. William L. Craig and Paul M. Gould (Wheaton, Ill.: Crossway, 2007), p. 63.

p. 62   Timothy Dwight's preaching on the truth of the Scriptures: Charles Cuningham, *Timothy Dwight, 1752–1817* (New York: Macmillan, 1942), p. 301.

p. 62   "their minds and consciences were moved": J. Edwin Orr, *Campus Aflame: A History of Evangelical Awakenings in Collegiate Communities* (Wheaton, Ill.: International Awakening Press, 1994), p. 40.

p. 63   "It has always been a sin not to love": Os Guinness, quoted in Noll, *Scandal of the Evangelical Mind*, p. 23.

Interlude: Reflections on Campus Foundations

p. 64   Augustine quoted in Kelly Monroe Kullberg, ed., *Finding God at Harvard* (Downers Grove, Ill.: InterVarsity Press, 2007), p. 290.

p. 67   That foundational relationship has been tested: Two indispensable works on this subject, especially focused on the history of faith and learning in the United States, are George M. Marsden, *The Soul of the American University* (New York: Oxford University Press, 1994), and James T. Burtchaell, *The Dying of the Light* (Grand Rapids: Eerdmans, 1998). Burtchaell's conclusion, while depressing, is piercing: "Religion's move to the academic periphery was not so much the work of godless intellectuals as of pious educators who, since the onset of pietism, had seen religion as embodied so uniquely in the personal profession of faith that it could not be seen to have a stake in social learning" (p. 842) and "these stories do imply that higher learning, if not an irresistible seducer, is still a very able one. The mind's affluence does seem at least as beguiling as that of the body. There was, in the stories told here, little learned rage against the dying of the light" (p. 851). An encouraging response to the work of Burtchaell, particularly addressing how colleges and universities can guard against the "the dying of the light" is Robert Benne, *Quality with Soul: How Six Premier Colleges and Universities Keep Faith with Their Religious Traditions* (Grand Rapids: Eerdmans, 2001).

p. 67   "priests who have lost their faith, and kept their jobs": Kelly Monroe Kullberg, "Introduction: Found by God at Harvard," *Finding God at Harvard*, p. 18.

Chapter 4: Praying Under a Haystack

p. 75   "A dark cloud was rising in the west": Byron Green, a letter describing the Haystack Prayer Meeting in 1806, quoted in Leverett Wilson Spring, *A History of Williams College* (Boston: Houghton Mifflin, 1917), pp. 78-79.

p. 75   "a heavy storm 'broke up the sunrise service' ": Spring, *History of Williams College*, pp. 186-87.

p. 76   "awkward figure . . . [with a] croaking sort of voice": Timothy Woodbridge, *Autobiography of a Blind Minister*, quoted in Clarence P. Shedd, *Two Centuries of Student Christian Movements* (New York: Association Press, 1934), pp. 49-50.

p. 76   "O that I might be aroused from this careless": Samuel Mills, quoted in John H. Hewitt, *Williams College and Foreign Missions* (Boston: Pilgrim Press, 1914), p. 41.

p. 76   "I shall have an opportunity to [pray] today": Samuel Mills, quoted in Spring, Memoirs of Samuel J. Mills, p. 21 <www .archive.org/details/Johns_Hopkins_University>.

p. 76   "These were part of a surge in student initiatives": Shedd, *Two Centuries of Student Christian Movements*, pp. 32-47; 61-90.

p. 77   "Perhaps no one finding": Ibid., p. 74.

p. 78   "foreign missionary society" was the most influential: Ibid., p. 73.

p. 78   established primary and secondary schools: J. Edwin Orr, *Campus Aflame: A History of Evangelical Awakenings in Collegiate Communities* (Wheaton, Ill.: International Awakening Press, 1994), pp. 53-60.

p. 79   College Day of Prayer: W. S. Tyler, *Prayer for Colleges* (New York: The Society, 1859).

p. 79   "students were doing much more than seeking for hints": Shedd, *Two Centuries of Student Christian Movements*, p. 75.

p. 79   "Epidemics tip because of the extraordinary efforts": Malcolm Gladwell, *The Tipping Point: How Little Things Can Make a Big Difference* (London: Abacus, 2001), p. 22.

p. 80   "Though you and I are very little beings": Samuel Mills, quoted in Spring, *Memoirs of Samuel J. Mills*, p. 25.

p. 80   "With [Samuel Mills] the field was the world": Hewitt, *Williams College and Foreign Missions*, p. 52.

Chapter 5: Sacred Space and Civil War

p. 87   "Human slavery is now doomed in the United States": Horace Bushnell, quoted in Orr, *Event of the Century*, p. 198.

p. 88   "the education of people of color": See Clarence P. Shedd, *Two*

Centuries of Christian Student Movements (New York: Association Press, 1934), p. 87.

p. 88   "conscientiously disband and relinquish the right": Anti-Slavery Society students, quoted in J. Edwin Orr, *Campus Aflame: A History of Evangelical Awakenings in Collegiate Communities* (Wheaton, Ill.: International Awakening Press, 1994), p. 62.

p. 88   God apparently visited everyone: Orr, *Event of the Century.*

p. 89   "Slavery is primarily the church's sin": Charles G. Finney, *Lectures on Revival* (Minneapolis: Bethany House, 1988), p. 189.

p. 89   "for the outpouring of the Spirit": G. A. Blackburn, *The Life Work of John L. Girardeau* (1899), quoted in Orr, *Event of the Century*, p. 40.

p. 89   "he stood speechless under the strange physical feeling": Ibid.

p. 90   "I am from Omaha, Nebraska": W. C. Conant, *Narrative of Remarkable Conversions* (1858), quoted in Michael F. Gleason, *When God Walked on Campus* (Dundas, Ont.: Joshua Press, 2002), p. 53.

p. 90   Samuel H. Fisher, James B. Reynolds and Henry B. Wright, *Two Centuries of Christian Activity at Yale* (New York: G. P. Putnam, 1901), p. 93, available online through the University of Toronto Libraries and accessed April 8, 2009, at <www.archive.org/details/twocenturieschr00wriggoog>.

p. 91   list of some of the campuses that were involved: See Orr, *Event of the Century*, pp. 177-191.

p. 91   At the start of the Civil War . . . 250 colleges: Frederick Rudolph, *The American College and University* (New York: Alfred A. Knopf, 1962), p. 47.

p. 92   "the discourse of reason, intelligence, and *faith*": W. W. Ferrier, *Origin and Development of the University of California*, p. 273, as cited in Orr, *Campus Aflame: A History of Evangelical Awakenings in Collegiate Communities* (Wheaton, Ill.: International Awakening Press, 1994), italics added.

p. 92   "The revival moved out to sea": Bob Eklund, "The 1858 Awakening," in *Spiritual Awakening* (Atlanta: Southern Baptist Convention, 1986), p. 28.

p. 92   "One of the first effects of the awakening": J. Edwin Orr, *The Second Evangelical Awakening in Britain* (London: Marshall, Morgan & Scott, 1949), p. 210.

p. 92   surge of interdenominational mission movements: Ibid., pp. 227-29.

p. 93   "The Civil War, as a consequence": Mark Noll, *The Old Religion in a New World: The History of North American Christianity* (Grand Rapids: Eerdmans, 2002), p. 109.

p. 93   "Why did not the 1857–1858 Awakening": Orr, *Event of the Century*, p. 216.

Chapter 6: Learning to Live for the Impossible

p. 98   "Has any such offering of living young men and women": John McCosh, president of Princeton University (1868–1888), quoted in Ruth Wilder Braisted, *In This Generation: The Story of Robert P. Wilder* (New York: Friendship Press, 1941), p. 30.

p. 99   "the source of the modern missionary uprising": Robert Wilder, *The Student Volunteer Movement: Its Origins and Early History* (1935), quoted in Keith Hunt and Gladys Hunt, *For Christ and the University* (Downers Grove, Ill.: InterVarsity Press, 1991), p. 43.

p. 99   "There never was a place": J. Edwin Orr, *Campus Aflame: A History of Evangelical Awakenings in Collegiate Communities* (Wheaton, IL: International Awakening Press, 1994), p. 101

p. 100   "Three or four days before the close": Timothy C. Wallstrom, *The Creation of a Student Movement to Evangelize the World* (Pasadena, Calif.: William Carey International Press, 1980), pp. 45-46.

p. 100   five students were chosen to travel: Clarence P. Shedd, *Two Centuries of Student Christian Movements* (New York: Association Press, 1934), pp. 264-65.

p. 101   The summer of 1887 "brought as an encore performance": Wallstrom, *Creation of a Student Movement*, p. 49.

p. 101   "They never asked of others": Braisted, *In This Generation*, p. 37.

p. 101   "I can truly answer that next to the decision": John Mott, quoted in *Witnessing to the Kingdom: Melbourne and Beyond*, ed. Gerald H. Anderson (Maryknoll, N.Y.: Orbis, 1982), p. 11.

p. 102   "He was an apostle of a simple Christianity": Herman Smitt Ingebretsen, "Nobel Peace Prize 1946 Presentation Speech," in *John R. Mott: That the World May Believe*, ed. Lon Allison (Wheaton, Ill.: EMIS, 2002), p. 85.

p. 102   "We also ask for love. *Give us friends*": V. S. Azariah, quoted in Anderson, *Witnessing to the Kingdom*, p. 25, italics added. For examples of the military language that often dominated Mott's addresses in the earlier days of the movement, see Wallstrom, *Creation of a Student Movement*, p. 65, and Michael T. Parker, "The Kingdom of Character: The Student Volunteer Movement for Foreign Missions" (Ph.D. diss., University of Maryland, 1994).

p. 103   "Christ has not revealed Himself solely": Allison, ed., *John R. Mott*, p. 51.

p. 103   Lamin Sanneh's research on missionaries: Lamin Sanneh, *Whose Religion Is Christianity? The Gospel Beyond the West* (Grand Rapids: Eerdmans, 2003).

p. 104   "Why is it important to see Jesus?": Robert Wilder, quoted in *The*

Evangelization of the World in this Generation, p. 24.

p. 104   "in seeing Jesus, they had seen the very face of God": For a wonderful introduction to the disciples' first-century understanding of who Jesus was, see N. T. Wright, *The Challenge of Jesus* (Downers Grove, Ill.: InterVarsity Press, 2000).

p. 104   SVM's three essential activities: Wallstrom, *Creation of a Student Movement*, pp. 56-58.

p. 104   "prayer and missions are faith and works": John Mott, "Prayer and the Missionary Enterprise," in *World-wide Evangelization* (New York: Student Volunteer Movement for Foreign Missions, 1902), p. 241.

p. 105   "[The] Movement owes everything to prayer": Mott, quoted in *John R. Mott*, pp. 41-42.

p. 105   "experience of consecration and spiritual renewal": Shedd, *Two Centuries of Student Christian Movements*, p. 261.

p. 106   "God is ready to give you the power": Braisted, *In This Generation*, p. 16.

p. 106   "The world has yet to see what God will do": Henry Varley, quoted in Lyle Dorsett, *A Passion For Souls: The Life of D. L. Moody* (Chicago: Moody Press, 1997), p. 141.

p. 106   Original student volunteers from Mount Holyoke: Wallstrom, *Creation of a Student Movement*, p. 79.

p. 107   "I never heard anyone speak of Jesus Christ as he did": Student speaking of Robert Wilder, quoted in Braisted, *In This Generation*, p. 119.

Chapter 7: Ivory Towers and Tongues of Fire

p. 113   John Oxenham was one of the pen names of William Arthur Dunkerley (1852–1941), an English journalist, poet and novelist who wrote *Bees in Amber*, which in time became a bestselling book of poetry. This particular poem is quoted in Dick Bohrer, *Bill Borden: The Finished Course, The Unfinished Task* (West Linn, Ore.: Glory Press, 1984), p. 91.

pp. 113-14   "I do not want you to think . . . ": Mrs. Borden, quoted in Mrs. Howard Taylor, *Borden of Yale '09: The Life That Counts* (London: China Inland Mission, 1926), p. 264.

p. 114   "Bill seems nearer and more gloriously living": Sherwood Day, quoted in Mrs. Howard Taylor, *Borden of Yale '09: The Life That Counts* (London: China Inland Mission, 1926), p. 264.

p. 114   "I cannot understand it!": Taylor, *Borden of Yale '09*, pp. ix-x.

p. 114   "genuine spiritual awakenings among students": "Missionary Review of the World, 1905," quoted in J. Edwin Orr, *Campus Aflame: A History of Evangelical Awakenings in Collegiate Communities*

(Wheaton, Ill.: International Awakening Press, 1994), p. 133.

p. 115   "I felt ablaze with a desire to go": Evan Roberts, quoted in J. Edwin Orr, *The Flaming Tongue* (Chicago: Moody Press, 1973), p. 5.

p. 115   "the tears freely flowed": Evan Roberts, quoted in Jessie Penn-Lewis, *The Awakening in Wales* (Fort Washington, Penn.: Christian Literature Crusade, 1993), p. 64.

p. 115   "The whole community was shaken": Ibid., pp. 66-67.

p. 116   The Welsh awakening produced supernatural phenomena: Orr, *Flaming Tongue*, pp. 15-19.

p. 116   Cornell, Rutgers, Mississippi State, Baylor, Stanford, Trinity: Orr, *Campus Aflame: A History of Evangelical Awakenings in Collegiate Communities* (Wheaton, Ill.: International Awakening Press, 1994), pp. 111-23.

p. 116   The honor system adopted in college examinations: Ibid., p. 125.

p. 117   "The entire room fell to their knees as fires of baptism ignited": Craig Borlase, *William Seymour* (Lake Mary, Fla.: Charisma House, 2006), p. 115.

p. 117   correspondence between Evan Roberts and Frank Bartleman: Frank Bartleman, *Azusa Street* (New Kensington, Penn.: Whitaker House, 1982), p. 15.

p. 117   "the land seems to be on the lookout": Orr, *Flaming Tongue*, pp. 65-68.

p. 118   "The color line was washed away at Azusa": Frank Bartleman, quoted in Borlase, *William Seymour*, p. 134; and Bartleman, *Azusa Street*, p. 56.

p. 118   "Some were crying, some dancing": Borlase, *William Seymour*, pp. 115.

p. 118   "For the record, I believe it actually happened": For a very readable and well-informed introduction to the phenomenon of speaking in tongues, see John Sherrill's classic *They Speak with Other Tongues* (Grand Rapids: Chosen Books, 1964). Sherrill's true story is particularly insightful because it was written from the perspective of an investigative journalist.

p. 119   effects of Azusa Street are 250 million worldwide: David Martin, *Pentecostalism: The World Their Parish* (Oxford: Blackwell, 2002), p. 1.

p. 119   "Is it possible to draw these extremes together": Pete Greig, founder of 24-7, in personal correspondence with me, June 4, 2008.

p. 120   Cecil Polhill-Turner's visit to Azusa Street: Orr, *Flaming Tongue*, p. 183.

p. 121   "Change, cleanse, use me as Thou shalt choose": William Borden, quoted in Taylor, *Borden of Yale '09*, p. 123.

p. 121   "He kept on, alone, and in response to his last prayer": Douglas Nelson, *For Such a Time as This*, describing the Azusa experience of William Seymour, quoted in Borlase, *William Seymour*, p. 119.

p. 122   Seymour (pronounced: See-More): Winkie Pratney, revival historian and humor icon, first pointed out the irony of Seymour's name to me.

Interlude: Reflections on Student Movements

p. 123   "Since Jesus' time numberless bands of Christian youth": Clarence P. Shedd, *Two Centuries of Student Christian Movements* (New York: Association Press, 1934), p. 1.

p. 124   by the 1920s "the evangelical Protestantism of the old-time colleges": George M. Marsden, *The Soul of the American University* (New York: Oxford University Press, 1994), p. 4.

p. 124   "Whereas before *character development* had been a primary aim": See Mark Noll, *The Scandal of the Evangelical Mind* (Grand Rapids: Eerdmans, 1994), pp. 110-14.

p. 125   SVM's numbers and focus faded: For more details on the decline of the SVM, see David Howard, *Moving Out: The Story of Student Initiative in World Missions* (Downers Grove, Ill.: InterVarsity Press, 1984), pp. 50-56; and Keith Hunt and Gladys Hunt, *For Christ and the University* (Downers Grove, Ill.: InterVarsity Press, 1991), pp. 39-55.

p. 125   SFMF chapters began to rapidly multiply: Howard, *Moving Out*, p. 61.

p. 126   "IVCF was a student mission, not a mission to students": Hunt and Hunt, *For Christ and the University*, p. 222.

p. 126   "I do not agree with Inter-Varsity in its theology": Ibid., pp. 78-79.

p. 126   Navigators' leadership encouraged them to partner: J. Edwin Orr, *Campus Aflame: A History of Evangelical Awakenings in Collegiate Communities* (Wheaton, Ill.: International Awakening Press, 1994), p. 191.

p. 127   "The Lord has done what I wanted Him to do this week": Jim Elliot, quoted in Elizabeth Elliot, *Through Gates of Splendor* (Carol Stream, Ill.: Tyndale House, 1996), p. 7.

p. 127   "He is no fool who gives what he cannot keep": Jim Elliot, quoted in Elizabeth Elliot, *Shadow of the Almighty* (San Francisco: Harper & Row, 1958), p. 15.

p. 127   Huaorani people group: These people were sometimes called the Auca. But Auca is a pejorative name given by neighboring tribes.

pp. 127-28   more than 250 UCLA students decided to follow Jesus: See "1951–1959" on the Campus Crusade For Christ International website <www.ccci.org/about-us/ministry-profile/timeline-1950s .aspx>.

p. 128   national directors of IVCF, NAV and CC were meeting together: Orr, *Campus Aflame: A History of Evangelical Awakenings in Collegiate Communities* (Wheaton, Ill.: International Awakening Press, 1994), pp. 191-92.

p. 128   YWAM was an organization "that sent kids out after high school": See the history section of YWAM's international website <www .ywam.org/contents/abo_his_1956.htm>. For more on YWAM's pioneering history, especially see Loren Cunningham, *Is That Really You, Lord?* (Seattle: YWAM Publishing, 2001).

p. 129   "God is at work on college campuses": John W. Alexander, quoted in Hunt and Hunt, *For Christ and the University*, p. 236.

Chapter 8: When History Is Ripe for Change

p. 136   "Come senators, congressmen": Bob Dylan, "The Times They Are A-Changin'," *The Times They Are A-Changin'* (1964).

p. 136   "You say you want a revolution": The Beatles, "Revolution" (1968).

p. 139   "This vital decision rests with the . . . reform-minded students": The Cox Commission Report, *Crisis at Columbia* (New York: Vintage Books, 1968), p. 197.

p. 139   "Uncle Milo's Nudist Farm": Nathan Johnson's debut album, *In Search of the Flip*, was followed by the innovative sounds of his critically acclaimed *Annasthesia*. For more, check out <www .thecinematicunderground.com> and <www.nathanj.com>.

p. 140   "It was easy to dismiss his behavior as a silly stunt": For a moving obituary of the legendary Naked Guy at Berkeley, who tragically committed suicide in 2006, see Jason Zengerle, "The Naked Guy," *New York Times*, December 31, 2006 <www.nytimes .com/2006/12/31/magazine/31naked.t.html>.

p. 140   "Nineteen sixty-eight had the vibrations of an earthquake": Lance Morrow, "Like a Knife Blade," in a 2008 fortieth anniversary special of *Time* titled "1968: The Year That Changed the World," p. vi.

p. 140   "such periods are referred to in terms of *kairos*": For New Testament usage of the word *kairos*, see Mk 1:14-15; Lk 12:54-56; 19:44; Rom 13:11-13; 2 Cor 6:1-2.

p. 141   "Those of you who are black can be filled with hatred": Robert Kennedy, quoted in Morrow, "1968: The Year That Changed the World," p. 5.

p. 142	"Mark Rudd's revolutionary letter to the administration": A full copy of Rudd's letter is provided in Avorn, *Up Against the Ivy Wall*, pp. 25-27.
p. 142	"Grudges are gone, prejudices forgotten": Coleman, *One Divine Moment*, pp. 97-98.
p. 143	"Utter honesty has been the standard": Ibid., p. 45.
p. 143	"the outstanding and inevitable mark of the college awakenings": J. Edwin Orr *Campus Aflame: A History of Evangelical Awakenings in Collegiate Communities* (Wheaton, Ill.: International Awakening Press, 1994), p. 217.
p. 143	"I lie so much I don't know when I'm lying": Kinlaw, *A Revival Account*, also available online YouTube <www.youtube.com/watch?v=7qOqitlKUNs>.
p. 144	"I have been keeping up the outward appearances": Coleman, *One Divine Moment*, p. 46.
p. 144	"my self-sufficiency was failing me": Ibid., pp. 46-47.
p. 145	"Jesus freaks. Evangelical hippies": "Street Christians: Jesus as the Ultimate Trip," August 3, 1970 <www.time.com/time/magazine/article/0,9171,876689,00.html>. For an excellent overview of the Jesus Movement as whole, see the June 21, 1971, *Time* cover story, "The New Rebel Cry: Jesus Is Coming!"
p. 145	"the hip scene was filled with plastic love": "Street Christians."
p. 146	"Much of the heat of the Jesus Movement": Malcolm McDow and Alvin L. Reid, *Firefall: How God Has Shaped History Through Revivals* (Nashville: Broadman & Holman, 1997), p. 316.
p. 147	"no idea that history was being made": Rosa Parks, quoted in "Daily Verse and Voice," *Sojourners,* May 11, 2009.
p. 147	"Let the circle of the offense be the circle": J. Edwin Orr, *Full Surrender* (London: Marshall, Morgan & Scott, 1951), pp. 27-28.

Chapter 9: Prayer Is the Place to Begin

p. 153	"Campus Ohio. The name is telling in its singularity": Ryan Milner, "Campus Ohio: A Report from Universities in the USA," *24-7 Prayer.com*, April 6, 2007 <www.24-7prayer.com>.
p. 154	See especially two papers by John Hayward, "Mathematical Modeling of Church Growth" (Technical Report UG-M-95-3, July 1995) and "A Dynamic Model of Church Growth and Global Revival" (Technical Report UG-M-00-4), presented at the annual meeting for the Scientific Study of Religion, October 18-21, 2000. For a very insightful perspective on the implication of Hayward's research, see Pete Greig, *Awakening Cry* (London: Silver Fish, 1998), pp. 111-22.
p. 154	interactive online map of the Swine Flu: See "Timeline of influ-

enza A(H1N1) cases," World Health Organization <www.who.int/csr/disease/swineflu/interactive_map/en/index.html>.

p. 155   "We pray for the big things, . . . we pray for the small things": Slate Stout, quoted in John Faherty, "Ariz. Students Organize Prayer Marathon," *USA Today*, November 2, 2007, <www.usa today.com/news/religion/2007-11-02-prayermarathon_N.htm ?POE=click-refer>.

p. 155   A sophomore overcame an eating disorder: Jillian Berman, "Student Groups Kick Off 40 Days of Prayer," *Michigan Daily*, January 14, 2008 <www.michigandaily.com/content/student-groups-kick-40-days-prayer>.

p. 155   "twenty campus groups were part of the prayer initiative": Veronica Menaldi, "Campus Christian Groups Unite for 40 Day Prayer Marathon," *Michigan Daily*, January 8, 2009 <www.mich igandaily.com/content/2009-01-09/campus-christian-groups-unite-40-day-prayer-marathon>.

p. 155   "When [an] employee decided to end his life": Sherri Williams, "Answered Prayers: Suicidal Man Persuaded to Live," *Columbus Dispatch*, February 10, 2008 <www.thecolumbusdispatch.com/live/content/local_news/stories/2008/02/10/samaritans_ou .html?sid=101> italics added.

p. 157   "Those that visited the room encountered a wall of prayers": Tyler J. McCall, "Reigniting Prayer: A Report from Gardner-Webb University," *24-7 Prayer USA*, March 10, 2008 <http://www.24-7prayer.us/index.php?option=com_content&task=view&id=135 &Itemid=114&PHPSESSID=7c8373593cce2713f05cd1687fd44eed>. Articles about each of the campuses mentioned in this and the preceding paragraph are available in the "News" section of the website <www.24-7prayer.us>.

p. 157   "Find out about prayer. Somebody must find out about prayer": Philip Yancey, *Prayer: Does It Make Any Difference?* (Grand Rapids: Zondervan, 2006), p. 11.

p. 158   "a solemn assembly of prayer for spiritual awakening": For more on 268, Passion and Oneday, see <www.268generation.com>.

p. 158   "have catalyzed tens of thousands of students": For more on The Call, Onething, Luke 18 Project and IHOP, see <www.thecall.com> <www.luke18project.com> and <www.ihop.org>.

p. 159   "We chose to chase after unity in the body": Theo Davis, "Forty Days of Prayer at the University of Arizona," *InterVarsity*, May 29, 2007 <www.intervarsity.org/studentsoul/item/prayer-tent>. See also "24/7 Prayer Movement at Arizona," *InterVarsity*, <www .intervarsity.org/news/24/7-prayer-movement-at-arizona>   and "Urbana 06: Live a Life Worthy of the Calling," *24-7 Prayer USA*,

January 12, 2007 <www.24-7prayer.us/index.php?option=com
_content&task=view&id=85&Itemid=114>.

p. 159   Pete Greig, "The Vision," <www.24-7prayer.com/resources/28>.
          See also Pete Greig, *The Vision and the Vow: A Call to Disciple-
          ship* (Orlando: Relevant Books, 2004).

p. 161   "When God intends great mercy for His people": Matthew Henry,
          quoted in Stuart Robinson, "Paying the Price of Revival," *Global-
          Christians,* 1992 <www.globalchristians.org/prayer/payprice.htm>.

p. 161   most widespread movement of prayer ever experienced: See, for
          example, the recent history of the Global Day of Prayer at www
          .globaldayofprayer.com, as well as the histories of continuous
          prayer taking place through works like 24-7 based in England
          (www.24-7prayer.com) and the International House of Prayer
          based in Kansas City (www.ihop.org). Further examples can be
          found in the prayer movements of Korea, such as Prayer Moun-
          tain (Yoido Full Gospel Church), and also the historic prayer meet-
          ings in Lagos, Nigeria, that have gathered together more than
          three million people at one time.

p. 161   "Perhaps you think that God will not hear": Charles Spurgeon,
          "Day 3, Adoption: The Spirit and the Cry," *Charles Spurgeon on
          Prayer: A 30-Day Devotional Treasury,* ed. Lance Wubbels (Lynn-
          wood, Wash.: Emerald Books, 1998).

Chapter 10: When Our Prayers Become Practical

p. 166   Number of college and university campuses: For recent figures
          on the number of campuses in the United states, see the U.S.
          Department of Education's "Number of educational institutions,
          by level and control of institution: Selected years, 1980-81
          through 2006-07" (available at www.nces.ed.gov/FastFacts/dis
          play.asp?id+84).

pp. 169-70 Numbers of college and university students: For current figures
          on U.S. student enrollment in tertiary level education, see
          "School Enrollment in the United States: 2006," issued by the
          U.S. Census Bureau in August 2008 (available at www.census
          .gov/population/www/socdemo/school.html) and also "Interna-
          tional Students in the U.S." published by the Institute of Interna-
          tional Education in November 2008 (available at opendoors.iie-
          network.org/page/113119). Specific numbers of college and
          university students worldwide are more difficult to accurately
          establish, but the international website of Campus Crusade, one
          of the largest student networks in the world, suggests 110 million
          as an approximate figure (see www.ccci.org/about-us/ministry-
          profile/what-we-do.aspx).

p. 170   "Where do the leaders in these realms come from?": Charles Ma-
          lik, *The Two Tasks* (Westchester, Ill.: Cornerstone Books, 1980), p.
          30.

p. 170   "Jesus-like engagement with the needs of the world": Pete Greig
          first mentioned to me the three areas of mission, mercy and
          marketplace.

p. 173   The spiritual disciplines: Two important books on this are Dallas
          Willard, *The Spirit of the Disciplines: Understanding How God
          Changes Lives* (San Francisco: HarperCollins, 1988), and Richard J.
          Foster, *Celebration of Discipline: The Path to Spiritual Growth*
          (San Francisco: HarperCollins, 1978).

p. 177   "Jesus invited his followers to also use the word *Abba*": "So you
          have not received a spirit that makes you fearful slaves," Paul
          explains in Romans 8:15-16, "Instead, you received God's Spirit
          when he adopted you as his own children. Now we call him,
          'Abba, Father.' For his Spirit joins with our spirit to affirm that we
          are God's children."

LIKEWISE. *Go and do.*

A man comes across an ancient enemy, beaten and left for dead. He lifts the wounded man onto the back of a donkey and takes him to an inn to tend to the man's recovery. Jesus tells this story and instructs those who are listening to "go and do likewise."

Likewise books explore a compassionate, active faith lived out in real time. When we're skeptical about the status quo, Likewise books challenge us to create culture responsibly. When we're confused about who we are and what we're supposed to be doing, Likewise books help us listen for God's voice. When we're discouraged by the troubled world we've inherited, Likewise books encourage us to hold onto hope.

In this life we will face challenges that demand our response. Likewise books face those challenges with us so we can act on faith.

likewisebooks.com